About This Book

Why is this topic important?

Because of the saturation level attained through technology (e.g., iPods, TiVO, electronic games, DVD viewers in cars, and games on telephones and other personal electronic devices), people are accustomed to being entertained wherever they go. That is why trainers and educators often struggle to find ways to maximize learning time while keeping learners engaged. They continually look for ways to get people in a classroom to interact appropriately and at the same time aid learning. This is why many trainers and educators turn to games and activities that can encourage group interaction, entertain, relate to a topic, or stimulate thinking.

What can you achieve with this book?

Through the fun and engaging techniques outlined in this book, you can encourage group interaction or present and review key topic concepts with learners. Whether you need an activity to gain attention, set the mood for learning, review key program elements, or just allow learners to discover ways to directly apply what they have experienced to their workplaces or other environments, there is an activity in this book to meet your needs. This is where *Creative Learning: Games and Activities That REALLY Engage People* can prove invaluable.

How is this book organized?

The games and activities in this book are divided into five sections that follow the chronology of many learning events: Getting Started, Re-Energizing the Brain, Interim Reviews, Transfer of Learning, and Ending on a High Note. Additionally, there is a Resources section at the back of the book that provides information on relevant books, websites, and vendors.

About Pfeiffer

Pfeiffer serves the professional development and hands-on resource needs of training and human resource practitioners and gives them products to do their jobs better. We deliver proven ideas and solutions from experts in HR development and HR management, and we offer effective and customizable tools to improve workplace performance. From novice to seasoned professional, Pfeiffer is the source you can trust to make yourself and your organization more successful.

Essential Knowledge Pfeiffer produces insightful, practical, and comprehensive materials on topics that matter the most to training and HR professionals. Our Essential Knowledge resources translate the expertise of seasoned professionals into practical, how-to guidance on critical workplace issues and problems. These resources are supported by case studies, worksheets, and job aids and are frequently supplemented with CD-ROMs, websites, and other means of making the content easier to read, understand, and use.

Essential Tools Pfeiffer's Essential Tools resources save time and expense by offering proven, ready-to-use materials—including exercises, activities, games, instruments, and assessments—for use during a training or team-learning event. These resources are frequently offered in looseleaf or CD-ROM format to facilitate copying and customization of the material.

Pfeiffer also recognizes the remarkable power of new technologies in expanding the reach and effectiveness of training. While e-hype has often created whizbang solutions in search of a problem, we are dedicated to bringing convenience and enhancements to proven training solutions. All our e-tools comply with rigorous functionality standards. The most appropriate technology wrapped around essential content yields the perfect solution for today's on-the-go trainers and human resource professionals.

www.pfeiffer.com

Essential resources for training and HR professionals

THIS BOOK is dedicated to several wonderful people who have influenced my life and allowed me to reach the point where I could write this book:

My wonderful wife M.J. and mother Rosie, both of whom support me and do so much that allows me to grow and be who I am;

My good friend Sylvia Foy, who gave her trust, wisdom, guidance, and encouragement to create a professional environment in which I was able to experiment and grow as never before when I was the training manager at the AAA national office. Many of the techniques and strategies included in this book are a direct result of her support; and

My business partner and friend, Steve Tanzer, who provides a sounding board for my many enthusiastic and sometimes offbeat ideas.

Pfeiffer™

Creative Learning

ACTIVITIES AND GAMES THAT *REALLY* ENGAGE PEOPLE

Robert W. Lucas

BICENTENNIAL
1807
WILEY
2007
BICENTENNIAL

John Wiley & Sons, Inc.

Library of Congress Cataloging-in-Publication Data
Lucas, Robert W.
  Creative learning : activities and games that really engage people / Robert W. Lucas.
    p. cm.
  Includes bibliographical references.
  ISBN 978-0-7879-8740-4 (pbk.)
  1. Adult learning. 2. Effective teaching. 3. Activity programs in education. I. Title.
  LC5225.L42L83 2007
  374—dc22
                        2007003998

Acquiring Editor: Martin Delahoussaye
Director of Development: Kathleen Dolan Davies
Developmental Editor: Susan Rachmeler
Production Editor: Dawn Kilgore
Editor: Rebecca Taff
Manufacturing Supervisor: Becky Carreño
Wiley Bicentennial Logo: Richard J. Pacifico

Printed in the United States of America

Printing   10   9   8   7   6   5   4   3   2   1

Contents

Game and Activity Usage Matrix

	Icebreaker	Energizer	Interim Review	Final Review	Team Building
1. Changing Paradigms		X	X	X	X
2. Silent Engagement	X	X	X	X	X
3. Sweet Anagrams	X			X	X
4. Fantasyland					
5. I Can Identify with That	X				
6. High Card	X	X			X
7. What Were You Doing	X	X			X
8. Meeting Nose to Nose	X				X
9. Scavenger Hunt	X	X	X	X	X
10. Making the Rules	X				X
11. Characteristic Card Swap	X				X
12. Who Am I?	X	X			X
13. Putting Your Memory to Work	X	X			X
14. Sentence Sense	X	X			X
15. Brain Teasers	X	X			X
16. Getting Down with the Sound	X	X	X	X	X
17. Cross-Laterals	X	X			X
18. What's My Issue?	X	X	X	X	X
19. Let's Get Together	X	X	X	X	X
20. Pass It Along	X	X			X
21. Team Scavenge	X	X	X	X	X
22. Macarena Coaching	X	X			X
23. Let Me Tell You a Story	X	X	X	X	X
24. Pass the Pickle		X	X	X	X
25. Balloon Review	X	X	X	X	X

Interpersonal Communication	Customer Service	Problem Solving	Decision Making	Visioning	Management/ Supervision	Train-the- Trainer	Orientation
X	X	X	X		X	X	X
X	X				X	X	X
X	X				X	X	X
				X	X		
X	X					X	X
X	X				X	X	
X	X				X	X	X
X	X				X	X	X
X	X				X	X	X
X	X		X		X	X	X
X	X	X			X	X	X
X	X				X	X	
X	X	X	X		X	X	X
X	X	X	X		X	X	
X	X	X			X	X	X
X	X	X	X		X	X	
X	X				X	X	X
X	X	X	X		X	X	X
X	X	X	X		X	X	X
X	X				X	X	X
X	X	X	X		X	X	
X	X				X	X	X
X	X	X	X		X	X	X
X	X	X	X		X	X	X
X	X	X	X		X	X	

(continued)

Game and Activity Usage Matrix *(continued)*

	Icebreaker	Energizer	Interim Review	Final Review	Team Building
26. Roll of the Dice		X	X	X	X
27. I've Got Your Number			X	X	X
28. Take a Pick		X	X	X	X
29. Let's "Eggs"amine This			X	X	X
30. My Present to You		X	X	X	X
31. Pop-Up Review			X	X	X
32. Name It			X	X	
33. Please Give Me a Hand			X		
34. It's Very Simple					
35. I Can Describe That					X
36. Putting Knowledge to Work					X
37. Words to Live By					
38. Content Shuffle			X	X	X
39. What if. . .?			X	X	X
40. A Puzzling Matter					X
41. Picture This					X
42. Verbal Volleyball			X		X
43. Pat on the Back			X	X	
44. Retention and Reaction			X	X	
45. A Postcard to Me			X	X	
46. We Can Sell This Idea			X	X	
47. Content Jeopardy			X	X	
48. Match It Up			X	X	
49. Concept BINGO!			X	X	
50. In Summary			X	X	
51. The ABCs of It All			X	X	
52. Concentration Review	X		X	X	

Interpersonal Communication	Customer Service	Problem Solving	Decision Making	Visioning	Management/ Supervision	Train-the-Trainer	Orientation
X	X	X	X		X	X	
X	X	X	X		X	X	
X	X	X	X		X	X	
X	X				X	X	
X	X	X	X		X	X	
X	X	X	X		X	X	
X	X	X			X	X	
					X		
X	X						
X	X				X		
X	X		X		X		X
	X	X	X		X	X	
X		X					
X		X		X	X	X	X
X		X	X		X	X	X
X		X					
X	X	X	X		X	X	X

Foreword

BOB LUCAS. The name introduces itself. Whether it's Bob's twenty-three books and publications, his Creative Presentation Resources materials, his many presentations at the ASTD International Conference and other like events, his earlier career work for AAA, his travels around the world, or even his stint as a Marine Corps drill instructor, Bob Lucas has been, and seems to be, everywhere. Even more importantly, Bob is right where he needs to be when it comes to the brain and learning. I discovered this when I first met Bob.

Actually, it took three attempts to meet Bob. The first attempt occurred when I was studying for my master's degree at Webster University. The university had posted information indicating that Bob would be the instructor for one class. I eagerly signed up. But alas, no Bob. The schedule was an old one issued by mistake, and the class had a different professor. The next time I almost met Bob was at one of his ASTD trainer conference presentations. Somehow, I misread the schedule and showed up for his session after it was over. Again, no Bob. The third time, finally and luckily, was the charm.

The main factor in the success of this introduction was that Bob sought me out. I was presenting my Show Biz Training presentation for an association in preparation for my own ASTD International Conference presentation. Bob was in the audience.

After the presentation, Bob approached me and struck up a conversation. For such a noted expert, this was a nice touch of humanity. As I talked to Bob, I discovered that he and I viewed the challenges of adult learning in like ways. Bob may have begun his career as a Marine Corps drill instructor, but when it comes to training, the one thing Bob does not act like is a drill instructor. He fully comprehends the need to reach trainees where they are, not to demand they go to you. Bob's ideas are brain-based, not order-based, and learner-focused, not instructor-centric.

I have since partnered several times with Bob. We presented together at two ASTD International Conferences. He has read and provided feedback on my works, as I have on his. To this day, we continue to exchange ideas and tips. Through all this communication, I have discovered Bob to be clearly focused on the needs of the learner and, as the many books that he has written superbly demonstrate, clearly focused on your needs too.

As Bob indicates in *Creative Learning: Games and Activities That REALLY Engage People*, people, being impatient, need information *now*. They do not want to engage in mindless activities that have been shoe-horned into a training program because they fit the trainer's need to conduct an activity at that place in the instruction. Those kinds of activities are trainer-driven, not learner-needed. With the increased need to do more, spend less, train effectively, and deliver stellar results, *Creative Learning: Games and Activities That REALLY Engage People* can help your learners teach themselves your material. Bob has created templates that will do the work for you. All you need to do is learn them, articulate them, stand aside, and let the learning flow.

If you're reading this foreword, you have either purchased *Creative Learning: Games and Activities That REALLY Engage People* or are considering purchasing it. If you have not purchased it yet, do so . . . now! You will then have the pleasure of knowing Bob. Better yet, your learners will have the benefit of his wisdom. Either way, you win.

Turn the page and meet the one and only Bob Lucas.

Lenn Millbower, BM, MA, The Learnertainment® Trainer

Preface

CREATING stimulating learning environments has proven time and again to enhance the ability of learners at all ages to attain, retain, and recall information far beyond the walls of a classroom. Many studies have been done on ways to maximize learning and retention in educational and training settings. In fact, various scientists did so much research on the effects of environment on learning, how the human brain processes information, and ways to successfully integrate various elements into a learning experience in the 1990s that the era is sometimes referred to as the "decade of the brain." What they, and subsequent researchers, have found is that the brain is a truly complex organ that performs at multiple levels and does not stop growing and learning with age, as once thought. Instead, through engagement of the senses and active involvement in the learning process, learners can potentially reach heights of learning, even into their senior years, that were previously unexplored or thought of. Much of what we know about how the human brain learns can be directly attributed to decades of research and to the modern technology that allows scientists and researchers to virtually peer into the brain as various stimuli are provided to test subjects. Equipment such as magnetic resonance imaging (MRI) and position emission tomography (PET) emit electrical and radio waves that can be used to track and record activity as the brain observes; reacts to sounds, color, movement, odors, and visual images; recalls or stores information; or reacts to emotional input. Pictures can be taken as a person's brain reacts to stimuli and the brain "fires" or shows activity in different areas. Such observations help better determine the types of functions that occur in various parts of the brain. This allows researchers to pinpoint mental functions related to learning. The observations also offer insights for trainers and educators into better strategies to help provide information and reinforce assimilation in the brain.

The importance of learner engagement can be seen by the proliferation of books and articles on accelerated or active learning that come on the market each year. Additionally, conferences and workshops, such as ASTD International, Training, International Alliance for Learning, Center for Accelerated Learning, and Eric Jensen's Learning Brain Expo, focus on strategies and techniques to teach educators and trainers ways in which strategies such as active learning, creativity, novelty, and fun can be incorporated into virtually any learning environment.

In my more than three-and-a-half decades of training adults, I have seen many changes in the way learning is approached in schools and organizations. Personally, I have changed my own perspectives based on research findings and have evolved from an autocratic "telling them" style, as a Marine Corps drill instructor in the early 1970s, to a die-hard "active training" zealot who uses a myriad of creative products and strategies in my classroom. In addition, I train others based on the lessons I've learned and sell hundreds of creative products designed to enhance learning environments. Does it all make a difference in learning? I believe that it absolutely does! I am not naïve enough to believe that using a whistle, putting handouts on colored paper, wearing a rubber animal nose, or playing a musical selection during a training event will cause learning to occur. However, I do continually see research that supports the possibility that such things as light, color, movement, sound, music, novelty, and various other elements can stimulate the brain and aid learning. For that reason I encourage their use. I also continue to get feedback from former trainees, colleagues, newsletter readers, and customers who tell me, "This stuff really works!"

As you read through this book, you will experience many of the activities that I have developed and modified over the years to engage learners and help ensure that true transfer of knowledge does occur. By gaining and holding attention through these games and activities, you can reinforce concepts that you are teaching, while at the same time add elements of fun to your learning event. I encourage you to use them as they appear or modify them as needed to get maximum effect. It is my hope that you will find as much value in using them as I have.

If you'd like to view over one thousand creative toys, games, and other learning-related products and get free ideas on how to enhance your learning environment, visit www.presentation resources.net. There, you can order products, read free articles on ways to enhance learning, and sign up for my free monthly newsletter. Additionally, if you have ideas for other activities that you'd like to share with me for possible inclusion in future books and my newsletter, or if you have questions about any of the activities in this book, please contact me at (800) 308–0399 or (407) 695–5535 or email me at blucas@presentationresources.net.

Best Wishes,
Bob Lucas

Acknowledgments

SPECIAL THANKS to the following people who helped make this book a reality:

Lenn Millbower, president of OffBeat Training and author of *Training with a Beat, Show Biz Training,* and *Cartoons for Trainers,* for his support and ideas in the past;

Martin Delahoussaye, senior editor at Pfeiffer, for his encouragement and support in developing the concept for this book and for providing ongoing guidance as the project progressed;

Julie Rodriguez, editorial assistant at Pfeiffer, for her coordination and support efforts that made bringing all the pieces of this project a little less stressful;

Susan Rachmeler, senior development editor at Pfeiffer, for her guidance, ideas, patience, and support in refining the manuscript and helping bring the final product to market; and Dawn Kilgore, senior production editor, for keeping track of the details as this project progressed.

Introduction

THERE ARE many books about games and activities for the learning environment. This one is different. All of the activities in this book focus on application of brain-based research and providing an enhanced learning environment and will work in engaging learners and enhancing the learning experience. *Creative Learning: Games and Activities That REALLY Engage People* also sets the background for successful use because, unlike most activities books that just provide the activities, this book highlights "how" each activity and game is related to brain-based research. As you read through this introduction, you will find many useful bits of information on the brain, on learning, and on how to get the most from this book.

While this book is not intended to provide an in-depth perspective related to research and theory behind adult and brain-based learning and related concepts, I have provided a cursory overview that is intended to pique your interest enough to have you go research more about the brain and how learning is potentially impacted by what you do in the classroom. Material on the use of light, sound, color, nutrition, movement, and smells and their relationship to learning environments can offer valuable insights into how the human brain processes information and things that you might do to incorporate these elements into your own training and educational settings. A listing of Resources on this topic can be found at the back of the book. In these resources, I have provided some vintage references (Knowles, Gardner, and others), since their work is the basis for what many trainers and educators do today, as well as some more current resources. Obviously, an Internet search of key terms like accelerated learning, brain-based learning, adult learning, creative training, and others will yield hundreds of other resources. I encourage you to explore such searches.

Rationale for This Book

Many trainers, educators, managers, and administrators view the use of games and activities as a frivolous waste of precious learning time—time that, in their minds, can be used more effectively by instructing learners and sharing knowledge in the old pedagogical manner. Some researchers have not found this to be true. Referring to games, puzzles, and toys, which come under the heading of brainteasers, Howard (2006, p. 654) states, "Games are helpful in maintaining flexibility in approaching problems. People who report that they enjoy and play these games also score higher on problem-solving tests." Yaman and Covington (2005, p. 20) address the use of game shows and state, "Game shows mix people up, force them out of their seats, and get them to participate . . . because they are involved, they become responsible for their own learning and for the training."

By using the games and activities found in this book, trainers, educators, and group facilitators will be able to tap a unique resource of techniques that can be used to gain and hold the attention of learners while setting an environment in which successful transfer of knowledge is more likely. That is because the activities found herein incorporate many of the elements that researchers suggest stimulate the brain, causing neurons, which are responsible for sending and receiving nerve impulses or signals, to fire and more effectively embed key learning concepts in the memory of participants. In many of the activities, you will find the use of novelty, fun, eustress (good stress) caused by time and other challenges, props, color, music, incentives, and various environmental elements crucial in helping the brain grasp and retain concepts. Eric Jensen of Jensen Learning (formerly The Brain Store) often suggests using such strategies and tools to better engage learners and enhance the learning process.

Games and Activities

Before I go any further, let's clarify what I mean by "games" and "activities."

What Are Games?

According to *The American Heritage Dictionary,* games are "an activity providing entertainment or amusement; a pastime." Further, the BrainyDictionary refers to games as, "A scheme or art employed in the pursuit of an object or purpose; method of procedure; projected line of operations; plan; project."

In training and educational settings, games may be commercial ones that have either been modified or reconfigured or simply used as designed. The goal in using such games is to teach learners real-life skills (for example, interpersonal communication, creativity, time and resource management, problem solving and decision making, change management, and team building). Games may also be developed by trainers or others specifically to address workplace and life issues. They typically follow rules and guidelines similar to those used to create their commercial relatives. Normally, this means that there are processes for starting and ending, determining the winner, scoring and/or rewarding participants, and creating an air of competition. Additionally, standard components/parts or equipment is used.

From a training and educational perspective, effective games should meet at least the following characteristics:

- *Meaningful.* At the very least, any game or other event used in training or education has to directly contribute to the program objectives and help learners gain new insights, knowledge, and/or skills. Failure to meet these criteria can create a situation in which valuable learning time is wasted and future management support for additional learning endeavors is potentially lost.

- *Time-Effective.* Games can range from a few minutes, such as the ones found in this book, to hours long, depending on the objective(s) and intent. The game or activity selected really depends on the time allotted for the session, the ultimate goal of the learning event, resources available, and expertise of the facilitator or educator. For example, I have been involved in, and have facilitated, short activities in which a specific point was being made. I have also attended one-day simulation games (for example, SIMSOC—Simulated Society) in which participants take on roles of different members of society and experience many challenges and emotions as part of the experience in order to raise awareness and compassion and encourage community involvement. In effect, the game and subsequent end-of-day processing was the learning experience.

- *Cost-Effective.* Most trainers and educators do not have unlimited resources or budgets for support materials. This is why the games and activities in this book offer various options. Most people can likely obtain either the primary or alternative suggested materials at little or no expense if they use their creativity. For example, depending on the organization (profit, not-for-profit, or non-profit) and focus, you may be able to get others to donate materials or items for your sessions.

- *Adaptable.* By using games that allow for flexibility or change, you will have a larger "tool box" of resources from which you can pull when you need games and activities. You always want to choose games that tie to your content and reinforce the message you are delivering. In this book, you often have a choice of formats and also different potential topic applications.

- *Non-Threatening.* Threats and intimidation are short-term motivators and are counterproductive. That is why any game you use in training or teaching others should be designed in a manner that celebrates successes and rewards learners rather than putting people in the position to fail or to be embarrassed. For this reason, you need to be aware of personal and cultural sensitivities—and possibly even allow people to opt out of participation in a game or activity if that seems appropriate. Built into many of the games and activities within this book are suggested rewards or incentives to assist in building a motivating learning experience while adding a bit of fun to the learning environment.

- *Participative.* The best games are those that involve people on a mental and emotional level. The more senses you can involve, the greater the chance they will "get it" and use what they learned later. Look for games that appeal to the three learning styles/modalities and as many of the multiple intelligences as possible.

In most sessions, your games and activities will be designed or adapted to supplement and reinforce your program objectives. That is what the games and activities in this book are designed to do.

What Are Activities/Exercises?

Activities or exercises (terms that are often used interchangeably by trainers and educators) are interactive events in which learners are challenged and engaged in their own learning. These events can be in the form of real-life simulations or role plays or other techniques in which they are encouraged to use actual or improvised materials. They often involve the use of such elements as novelty, time, props, music, and creativity.

Activities share many of the same characteristics as games. While some may involve the use of props or other materials, others (brief stretching activities) do not. They are typically used to accomplish such things as energize, relax, motivate, cause reflection, and teach concepts.

The Importance of Games and Activities in Learning

Like any other learning strategy, activities and games should be designed and used with the ultimate goal of reinforcing key elements of a learning event or engaging learners in order for them to better work toward attaining information, understanding concepts, or melding as a team. Games and activities should not be purely entertainment. Learning objectives must be defined, and these must be attained. These objectives might focus on team cohesiveness, enhanced communication, problem solving, or other workplace-related issues.

Some researchers suggest that using games and similar methods to share or expand knowledge in the classroom is an excellent way to help learners move concepts from the classroom into their long-term memory. Through repetitive activities, you can reinforce key concepts better than just by explaining them and moving on. Many trainers and educators use tools such as games and puzzles to create learning events during which students or participants can personally take ownership for part of their learning. Through such activities, learners are able to immediately reinforce concepts in memory and apply what they experience in the classroom in an upbeat, fun manner.

Part of the effectiveness of games and activities comes from tapping into early life experiences. At those times in life, many people learned to play games as a form of entertainment and enjoyment, without realizing that they were actually learning key life skills and knowledge in the process. Think about it. When you were a child playing games like Monopoly®, UNO®, Risk®, Clue®, Dominoes®, Life®, cards, and Parchisi®, did you think about the fact that you were using deductive reasoning, resource management, strategic planning, and other skills that you would later find a use for in the workplace and in life? You likely did not. You were probably just laughing, enjoying your friends, snacking on junk food, and having FUN! This prior experience and emotion can easily be recaptured through well-planned and executed classroom events. By encouraging learners to relax, laugh, and enjoy the experience, you can affect learning.

In fact, many of the common commercial games mentioned above can be adapted to accomplish your learning goals if you just plan a bit. Similarly, crosswords and word search puzzles can be excellent vehicles for reminding learners of key concepts and terms and for testing their memory or cognition in non-threatening and innovative ways. I regularly use word search puzzles as interim reviews (done throughout a session) and at the end of programs to cause learners to recall and reflect on key program terminology or elements. These tools can also be excellent icebreakers and pre-tests to get learners thinking about what they are going to experience in the learning event. One nice thing about them is that they can be created using inexpensive software you purchase (see Creative Presentation Resources in the Resource section) or find on the Internet.

The Relationship of Games and Activities to Brain-Based Learning

One of the added benefits of using interactive approaches in learning environments is that, in addition to actively involving learners and getting them to work with one another, you can potentially engage them on an emotional level by adding an element of excitement through friendly competition, time limits, activity, movement, and sound. Through laughter, you may stimulate the flow of blood to the brain, which in turn releases substances such as endorphins. This can help stimulate the neurons in the brain and increase the opportunity for learning to occur. Additionally, such techniques can set the stage for enhanced comprehension while adding an element of novelty, energy, and fun to goal attainment.

Many games and activities, by their nature, capture learner attention through one or more of the natural learning styles or modalities that people use (visual, auditory, or kinesthetic). They also potentially engage the brain from both hemispheres, which some researchers say control different bodily functions and actions—left (analytical) and right (creative). Some common functions attributed to each brain hemisphere include the following:

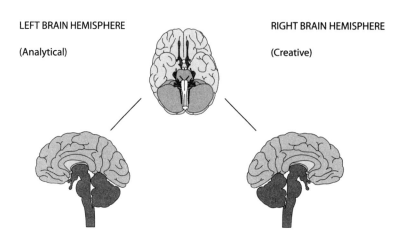

LEFT BRAIN HEMISPHERE

(Analytical)

RIGHT BRAIN HEMISPHERE

(Creative)

Left-Brain (Sequential [Parts] Processing)	Right-Brain (Random [Wholes] Processing)
Analytical	Intuitive
Verbal/language	Visualizes
Logical	Spatial
Sequential/linear processing	Spontaneous
Temporal	Holistic (learns whole/then parts)
Mathematical functions	Nonverbal processes
Prefers structure/predictability	External focus
Internal focus	Prefers to see/experience
Reasoning	Dreams
Judgments	Sees similarities
Deals with one thing at a time	Integrates multiple inputs

Depending on their form and focus, games and activities tap into many of the eight multiple intelligences identified by Harvard professor of education Howard Gardner (1993, pp. 17–26). Gardner actually introduced seven intelligences and later added the eighth. Throughout this book you will see references to these intelligences as you review the games and activities provided.

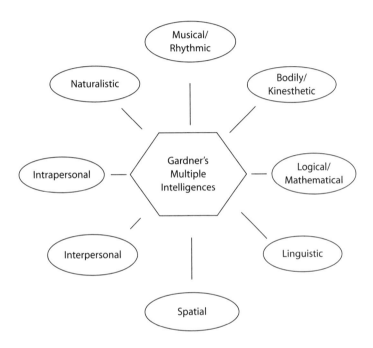

The eight multiple intelligences include:

1. Musical/Rhythmic Intelligence—allows someone to create or compose music and to understand, interpret, and appreciate it.

2. Bodily/Kinesthetic Intelligence—gives the ability to solve problems or manipulate items using one's own body or parts of the body.

3. Logical/Mathematical Intelligence—involves the ability to reason, calculate, think in a logical manner, and process information.

4. Linguistic Intelligence—is the ability to read, write, and communicate effectively in a variety of ways.

5. Spatial Intelligence—the ability to think in pictures and to visualize a conclusion or result.

6. Interpersonal Intelligence—is crucial for understanding others, their emotions, traits, and abilities, and how best to interact with people.

7. Intrapersonal Intelligence—provides the ability to form accurate perceptions about oneself and use the knowledge to effectively function throughout life.

8. Naturalistic Intelligence—gives the ability to observe, understand, and classify patterns in nature.

Debriefing

On his website, Dr. Sivasailam "Thiagi" Thiagarajan, a noted game expert, states that one should, "Use training games, simulations, and role plays that add an emotional element to learning." He does caution that one should: "Make sure that emotions don't become too intense and interfere with learning. Make sure that participants don't learn dysfunctional behaviors because of intense emotions. Debrief participants after emotional activities to reflect on their feelings and learn from their reactions." Thiagi's guidance is well-placed, since the goal in learning is to ultimately improve knowledge and performance. This is why a crucial element when using games and activities is to effectively debrief, process, or bring closure at the end of the event. This involves such strategies as questioning learners to have them reflect on what they experienced and tying in the learning outcomes of the activity to the program objectives. Additionally, debriefing helps bridge the gap between classroom concepts and the real world by helping learners to see direct applications in the workplace to what they have learned through the game or activity. You will note that each of the games and activities found in this book has a section related to effectively debriefing learners or reviewing the process they used.

Adding Props and Noisemakers

Games and activities can often be enhanced through the use of props and noisemakers. To find out where to find many of those mentioned in this book, consult the Resources section at the end. You can also use your own creativity and look for alternative items in toy stores, discount, clearance, or department stores (BIG Lots/Odd Lots, Kmart, Target, or Wal-Mart), online at www.ebay.com, party stores, teacher supply stores, or anywhere you can find toys or other products that can be modified to meet your specific training needs. The key is to think outside the box and always ask yourself, "What content concepts could I teach with this?" I often take what I call "idea excursions" and wander through different stores, picking up things and pondering how they could be used to make a specific point or present a concept in a novel way. It is a fun mental exercise, and I walk away with dozens of new product and program ideas. Try it.

Including Music in Your Activities

Research supports music usage in learning. An important study (Rauscher & Ky, 1993) was conducted related to the impact of music on the brain. This experiment resulted in what has been termed the "Mozart IQ effect" because Mozart's music was selected for use in the study. During the research, students at the University of California, Irvine, listened to relaxation music, Mozart, or white noise for ten minutes as they performed spatial tasks. Afterward, it was determined that those listening to Mozart outperformed others. This should not be construed to mean that listening to a certain type of music will result in accelerated or increased learning, since each person is different and reacts differently to various types and amounts of stimuli. It does mean that the potential for learning is there when using certain types of music.

Eric Jensen (2000) points out that, while this study alone cannot adequately cement the conclusion that listening to music was the reason for improved performance:

- The effect also occurs in rats exposed to music.

- People with epilepsy also show increased spatial reasoning.

- Twenty-seven studies replicating the original resulted in at least some positive "Mozart effect."

- Subjects of electroencephalogram (EEG) studies who listened to Mozart and then performed spatial-temporal tasks showed enhanced brain activity, compared to a control group that listened to a short story.

While there is controversy about the strength of the Mozart effect, there seems to be little doubt that music can positively impact brain functioning. Many researchers believe that it is not the type of music played, but rather the melody, harmony, and rhythm that influence the brain. Jensen (2005) lists ten reasons to use music, from increasing social contact to energizing a group.

Interestingly, as researchers are documenting the value of music for brain development, many school systems are cutting extra-curricular activities such as choir or band programs, or what they call "fluff," from school budgets. Recent discoveries suggest that the right type of music incorporated into a learning environment can reduce anxiety and stress, impact physiology, influence mood, and potentially aid learning.

Effectively Using Music

Like any other learning aid, musical selections during individual and group activities should be loud enough to be heard, but low enough not to distract or interrupt concentration or conversation. While some learners will enjoy the music and find it helpful, others might find it distracting and irritating. Do an in-class survey periodically to see how learners are doing during activities. Ask them what you can do to help them be more effective. Someone may tell you to turn the music off. If this occurs, survey all learners to see if that is the consensus and act accordingly. If you do leave it on, suggest that researchers have found that many people benefit from such stimulation. The bottom line is that you have to decide on a case-by-case basis whether the music is really needed and helpful. Don't use it just because you like it.

For background music, you are probably better off using nature sounds or instrumental selections, new age, or classical, instead of vocals, so that participants do not subconsciously focus on the words and sing along in their heads. To benefit most from using music in your sessions, some research suggests that you choose selections that have approximately forty to sixty beats per minute if you want to slow the pace of activity, for individual work, visualization activities, or relaxation. This is because that pattern of sound will mimic the average person's heart rate and will be in sync with his or her natural rhythm. If you want to stimulate creative thinking and assist in problem solving, increase the tempo to sixty to seventy beats per minute. Finally, if you want to really energize participants and get them moving (for example, during fast-paced activities, while exercising, or when moving them from one place to another), use music that has seventy to 140 beats per minute.

As a trainer or educator, you can add music to the background to break the awkward silence that sometimes exists as participants enter the room or return from breaks. You can also use music to signal the end of one event and the beginning of another. This works because the abrupt silence that occurs when the music is turned off attracts attention. Nonverbally, you are signaling that something is about to happen or that it is time to begin.

Music can definitely assist in setting the tone for a session and, if used correctly, can actually contribute to the theme. For example, in a class on time management, I use an hour of "oldies" songs that have the title or theme of time ("Time Won't Let Me" by the Outsiders, "Time Has Come Today" by the Chambers Brothers, and "Time in a Bottle" by Jim Croce). I play the songs as learners arrive and during breaks. In my opening remarks, I comment about how time influences every aspect of our lives, including our music. In another session, this one on motivation, I run in from the back of the room with the theme of the movie *Rocky* blaring away. Once in front of the class, I cut the music and in animated fashion welcome everyone with a loud, "GOOD MORNING! ARE YOU READY TO LEARN SOME TECHNIQUES TO IMPROVE YOUR WORK LIFE?" I get everyone to stand up and lead them through a fast-paced stretching or other fun activity. That leads to a small-group brainstorming activity about what gets people pumped up in today's workplace. We review their ideas and move into the program content.

Considerations When Selecting Music

When selecting music for your programs, do not forget that each participant has preferences related to music type (rock, rap, new age, and country), format (instrumental versus singing), and volume level. Also, recognize that some people will enjoy the music and others will complain about it. When making selections, experiment with different types to find a happy medium and ask for participant input. You may even want to discuss the issues mentioned in this section related to music and learning at the beginning of the session. Depending on how much music you plan to use, build in little competitions where the winner gets to assume the role of disc jockey who selects the next piece of music you will play. This is a fun way to involve participants and give them some control.

Because of the diverse nature of today's world and the likelihood that your learning group will come from various cultural, racial, ethnic, and geographical backgrounds, you must take these factors into account when selecting music for your learning events. Lenn Millbower (2000) points out the need for cultural awareness related to music usage by explaining the role of music in different parts of the world: "Music fulfills different needs in diverse locations around the world, and we are all prisoners of our cultural assumptions. Individuals, even professional musicians, have a difficult time appreciating the nuances of music outside their heritage. Erroneous music placement based on mistaken cultural assumptions is a potential source of embarrassment when training with music. You must know the cultural assumptions and expectations of your audience before selecting material" (pp. 134–135). The key to selecting the right type of music is to consider the organizational culture, topic, geographic location, and cultural background of learners. For example, while upbeat country and western music might play well as break music for a session being taught in Texas or other parts of the Western United States, it might not be well received in major cities of the Northeastern part of the country or in other countries. Because of the potential controversy about the song "YMCA" by the Village People, the music might not work well in the "Bible belt" section of the United States or other areas where strong religious convictions are predominant. Similarly, heavy metal or modern rock might generate frowns from an audience of fifty-plus corporate executives. To help select the music best suited for your needs, I have provided a starter list under Suggested Music in the Resources section. I also recommend Eric Jensen's books *Music with the Brain in Mind* and *Top Tunes for Teachers* and Jeff Green's *The Green Book of Songs by Subject,* both of which give hundreds of ideas related to the type of songs that can aid various training and educational activities.

Another point to remember is that you should not make music a major part of your program. Like any other training aid, music should be used to support your material and delivery, not substitute for it. Keep its use to a small portion of total learning time and use it to complement content, unless your program is about music.

Using Rewards or Incentives

Some educators and trainers would argue that rewards (candy, small prizes, rounds of applause, ribbons, stickers, and so on) are a waste of time and do little to stimulate involvement and achievement. Many times, their opinions are based on the type of training or topic that they facilitate, their professional environments and the people working there, their personalities, their prior experiences in seeing someone use such items, and, in some cases, their experience and ability to effectively manage multiple activities or techniques in a classroom. Others might argue that using such rewards is a great way to encourage interaction and positive behavior and that, by recognizing involvement and achievement, you can encourage similar repeated behavior in the future. Based on over three decades of using such techniques in my training and educational settings, I tend to be a believer. At the same time, I recognize that using rewards in a haphazard manner, not related to a topic or theme, or just for the sake of readily passing out "stuff" is probably not a good idea. Additionally, a trainer or educator planning to use rewards must be comfortable passing them out in an effective manner, just as they would be with using training aids and other materials during a session, so that their efforts look polished and professional, rather than like an afterthought.

Throughout this book, I have incorporated the use of rewards and applause following activities. I encourage this when someone volunteers by answering a question or otherwise becomes involved or is randomly selected to take a leadership or active role (for example, as a group leader or scribe). I believe that by rewarding people you can encourage others to become actively involved in their learning process. If you choose not to use individual rewards and simply have a round of applause after an activity, that is obviously your choice.

If you do decide to involve learners and use rewards, it is crucial to recognize that some people are more introverted or prefer to remain in the background. For that reason, I often randomly select "volunteers" (see Creatively Selecting Volunteers later in this Introduction), but give them an option to opt out of a role if they prefer, rather than making them uncomfortable. Failing to allow an opportunity to opt out could actually backfire on you and cause behavior problems and resentment, thus shutting down learning. This is why you want to monitor nonverbal cues closely throughout any learning activity and act accordingly.

From a learner's perspective, each is unique in his or her need or desire for rewards (consider what Abraham Maslow found in his historic research for the Hierarchy of Needs).

Some will view small toys and candy or applause as frivolous, while other will appreciate such recognition. I use all of these techniques and more to encourage involvement in my sessions and to add a bit of novelty and fun to a learning event. Some people appreciate and welcome incentives during a session, while others are more complacent. I believe that reluctance is often based on their previous learning experiences and expectations, combined with their personality types. My experience has been that, even in sessions with executives, some learners may initially balk at the idea of receiving such things as a smile face sticker on a name tent each time they volunteer to lead a group, take notes, or answer a question, but eventually they become competitive and will point out the fact that they "did something" worthy of a sticker should I fail to award one. I attribute this to their Type A personalities kicking in and their not wanting to be the only person without a sticker at the end of the day. This is especially true when I've had directors, managing directors, and vice presidents in a room together.

By the way, when I give stickers, playing cards, carnival tickets, or other small incentives throughout a session, I typically use them as a way of determining who gets a "grand prize" at the end of a session (for example, an autographed copy of one of my books or some session-related item). Throughout the session, participants collect the small incentives for involvement. The collective high or low total at the end of the day determines who gets a prize. By doing this, I give everyone an opportunity to be recognized during the session, I encourage individual participation, and I recognize overall accomplishment at the end of the learning event. Any prizes given are best if tied to the session theme or topic (for example, smile face items for customer service training, puzzles for problem-solving/decision-making groups, and computer toys for technical sessions) in order to reinforce the concepts once learners leave the classroom.

One final thought on rewards—-there should be no losers in learning environments. I make sure that everyone in the room leaves with some sort of prize. This can be easily accomplished through a "random" selection of volunteers and by recognizing any type of accomplishments that are made by any learner.

Additional Considerations

The number of people who have some form of disability rises each year as societies age around the world. For that reason, when designing any training activity or setting up a learning environment, you must be conscious of learners who might have an impairment that could prevent them from performing certain tasks. Always try to determine special needs in advance of a learning event or at least plan alternatives for each event so that every learner has equal access to information and can be involved at some level.

Creatively Forming Groups Using Props and Toys

Why Group Learners?

Actively engaging learners can add fun, novelty, and functionality to any session. By grouping learners, you can combine collective knowledge and ideas while helping to enhance the learning experience for all concerned. However, to do this you should consider the activities that you plan to use and the number of groups you will need for a given activity before a session actually begins. Once you decide on group number and size, you are ready to select group members using props or toys in any manner you can imagine. The value of selecting group members in this fashion is that you can make the choice of which learners end up in a group appear to be entirely random, even though you actually plan which learners work together. For example, if you know that certain individuals have a level of knowledge about a given subject that will be useful during a group activity and you want to make sure that they are equally divided among the groups, just ensure that each gets a different type of toy or prop so that they will be dispersed evenly among other learners. Random dispersion also helps to separate friends or co-workers who tend to congregate together, often resulting in side conversations and distractions and reducing networking opportunities for all learners.

Using Props and Creativity to Form Groups

Many techniques can be used to group learners. However, since this book is focused on games and activities, I have only included one of my favorite techniques below—using props and creativity to form groups. If you'd like more ideas, take a look at my book *The Creative Training Idea Book: Inspired Tips and Techniques for Engaging and Effective Learning.*

To introduce learners to the concept of using props and other random techniques for grouping, you may want to emphasize at the beginning of a session that "We'll be using a variety of toys, games, and incentives today to add a little FUN to the session." If you put these items on tables before they arrive, point them out to learners as part of your introductory remarks.

You may also want to explain that the items placed on tables may be kept by learners as a memento at the end of the session. In this way, you have functionality and reward rolled into one. Also, most learners will take these items back to their workplaces or homes and put them near their workstations or somewhere else where they are likely to see them frequently. Each time they do, the session and its content will normally come to mind to some degree, thus reinforcing learning.

The following are some of the items that you may want to use to group learners based on your session topic and desired outcomes. Many of these items can be purchased at teacher supply, party, toy, or novelty stores and through other venues listed in the Resources section at the back of this book.

Erasers

Brains can be used for sessions tied to such topics as learning (train-the-trainer), creativity, thinking outside the box, problem solving, or decision making.

Computers are perfect for software/PC training.

Crayon erasers can help focus attention of self-improvement or goal setting (for example, color your world).

Dinosaurs work well when teaching change programs (reluctance to change).

Food shapes can be used for restaurant/food services training or nutrition.

Ice cream cones relate to "licking the competition" or motivation.

Jungle animals are great for stress and time management (especially if you can find ones in the shape of monkeys—to illustrate "keeping the monkey off your back").

Light bulbs enhance creativity and brainstorming sessions.

Numbers and letters of the alphabet work for any topic area.

Police badges or hats are good for law enforcement or security training or sessions related to legal issues.

Sailboats, cars, planes, or trains expand the theme in travel/transportation classes.

Seasonal erasers can be used during a specific holiday season (Christmas, Valentine's Day, St. Patrick's Day, or 4th of July) or on a special day (Halloween—ghosts, Thanksgiving—turkeys, Easter—bunnies) just to add a festive note.

Star shapes tie nicely into motivation or customer service ("You're a star").

Telephones are great for telephone skills and customer service training.

Thumbs-up symbols are perfect for sessions or activities related to goal achievement, success, or strategic planning.

Wild animals can be used in diversity training to stress differences and at the same time strengths and similarities (for example, all species have certain things in common).

Stickers

Animals can be associated with many topics or industries (for example, "heart of a lion," "stealth of a cat," or "strong as an ox").

Cars and trucks can support classes for the automotive or travel industry or related topics.

Clock faces tie to time management or sessions where time is stressed.

Clown faces can add fun to humor training or other sessions in which you want to lighten the mood and add color.

Computers can be used in PC or technical skills training sessions.

Eyes can relate to optical industry classes or to stress "keep your eyes open."

Food shapes can relate to many types of restaurant and food services training.

Mouths and lips are perfect for nonverbal or verbal communication skills.

Safety or traffic signs can reinforce OSHA or workplace safety issue training, following the rules or regulations, obeying guidelines, policies or procedures.

Seasonal stickers can be used for any type of training based on a special day (St. Patrick's Day, Halloween, or New Year's).

Smile faces tie to virtually any industry or class (for example, customer service).

Stars can be used in any type program or when you want to stress "reach for the stars" with goal attainment.

Teeth and mouths can tie to dental classes or when you want to stress "sink your teeth into. . . ."

Traffic signs can focus attention on transportation and safety training or tie to sessions on driving.

Small Toys

Back scratchers made of wood or plastic can be related to ways of "reaching" or attaining a goal.

Chickens can be used for a theme (for example, "Don't be a chicken. . .") or for restaurant or industry-specific training.

Currency or coins are effective for bank teller or cashier training.

Ducks made of rubber or plastic might be used to remind people that sometimes things are not what they are "quacked up" to be (when discussing problems or how things can go wrong in a specific situation).

Fish exemplify successful programs/projects when things are "swimming along."

Footballs, baseballs, sponge balls, or similar small items may help emphasize teamwork or "getting on the ball."

Hand-held pencil sharpeners can point out the need to ask direct questions or "get to the point" when doing a customer service or interpersonal communication program.

Insects or bugs help in activities when discussing pet peeves or things that "bug" participants, either in customer interactions or the workplace world.

Puzzles to focus on problem solving, decision making, creativity, or putting things together (for example, setting up systems).

Smile-faced items can be used for customer service programs or virtually any other topic (for example, stuffed animals, hacky sacks, or foam balls).

Spinning tops made of plastic can emphasize high sales or improvement levels (on top of the world).

Zoo animals can add fun to virtually any subject or when discussing stress or a high-energy topic when things are hectic (for example, "It's a zoo around here").

Other Items

Colored markers can be used to add visual variety and to put symbols, letters, numbers, or other identifiers on name tents or nametags to designate team members.

Pencil sharpeners in different shapes and colors can be used to tie to themes (for example, light bulb sharpeners can tie to creativity).

Rubber stamps with different images or shapes on them (for example, smile faces, celestial bodies, animals, or vehicles) are perfect for tying to themes of your session or activity and can be customized at art/craft stores or those specializing in the stamping hobby.

Themed or colored pencils that offer a variety of sayings or colors can also be used to group learners and can be functional to allow note-taking during the session.

Creatively Selecting "Volunteers"

Trainers and educators can set the stage for participants to play an active role in the program by spending time at the beginning of a session talking about the roles of leader (spokesperson) and scribe (note-taker). It also helps when you plan to give small incentives (buttons, toys, candy, or other fun items) to your "volunteers" and let them know this at the beginning. Doing so can actually generate some friendly competition and enhance motivation as learners rush to volunteer throughout the day.

Why Assign Roles to Learners?

Why use a system for randomly selecting learners to take on specific roles during a session? For one thing, you can reduce the likelihood that one or two people will dominate or control the session, discussions, and activities. You also encourage interaction and input by all participants. Additionally, you disperse some of your administrative and monitoring duties.

Selection Strategies

Trainers and educators can select learners to perform tasks in hundreds of ways that are limited only by the creativity of the session facilitator. For example, there are numerous personal traits or characteristics that can be used to designate learners for specific groups or tasks. Think outside the box when looking for ways to assign roles and have fun with the process. However, be cautious not to choose something that will embarrass an individual, such as a physical characteristic that the person has no control over (nose/shoe size, weight, height, or eye/hair color). You should also be conscious not to focus on specific clothing, grooming styles, or other characteristics or items related to a group to which a learner belongs (religion, sexual preference, or race). Failure to remember the latter could potentially lead to charges of discrimination or preferential treatment.

Some more acceptable possibilities for selecting adults include:

- Person who traveled farthest/least to get to the program location

- Person wearing the most of an item or designated color

- Person with the most coins

- Person with the most/least pets

- Person most recently engaged or married

- Person with the fattest cat/dog

- Person with the most/least siblings

- Person who most recently washed a car

- Person with longest middle name

- Person with most/least letters in first name

- Person who has most recently attended another professional development program or academic class

- Person who most recently purchased a particular item (car, electrical appliance, piece of clothing)

- Person who most recently went to a dentist

- Birth date closest to/farthest from the date of your program

- Longest/shortest time with organization

- Person with decorative metal on shoes

- Person who most recently visited a hair stylist or barber

- Person who has most recently participated in an athletic event

- Person who has had the most cups of coffee/tea/juice since arriving at the session

- Person born in the city in which the program is being conducted

How This Book Is Organized

This book is designed to be a quick reference guide that can provide easily understood and useable resources for trainers, educators, or any group leader. It is designed with the idea that someone might pick up the book looking for a specific type of activity, rather than reading it cover to cover. This is why the same format is repeated from one activity to another.

The games and activities are easy to set up and facilitate, and time lengths vary to suit different learning environment needs and instructor preferences. The Resources section at the end provides many strategies, books, websites, and other resources that are useful in facilitating games and activities, as well as providing ideas for other learning environment adaptations.

Here's what you will find in each section of this book:

Use Matrix

Following the Contents, you will find a handy matrix that lists all the activities and games found in the book and identifies the potential use(s) for each game. Most will appear under multiple categories since they can be modified, adapted, or used at different times during various sessions to address various learning objectives.

Introduction

This section sets the tone for using the book by providing the research behind the use of games and activities and how they tie to brain-based learning and research. It also provides detailed ways in which you can most benefit from the book's content and enhance learning.

Section 1: Getting Started

In this section, you will find a variety of games and activities designed to help you identify ways in which you might open your sessions and classes on a high note, get things moving related to program content, and have people introduce themselves in fun and interesting ways.

Section 2: Re-Energizing the Brain

The content of this section is focused on raising and maintaining participant energy, motivation levels, and attentiveness related to learning and course content. From a learning standpoint, this is important because, for the human brain to grasp and assimilate concepts into memory, people must first be focused on stimuli (for example, information being presented, audiovisual aids, support materials, and other crucial components of the learning environment).

Section 3: Interim Reviews

Interim reviews are fun and beneficial steps in the learning process. They provide quick ways to help learners better grasp and retain session content for later recall and application. They also help facilitators identify any content that needs further attention and emphasis. Too often trainers and educators wait until the end of a learning event to review content. At that point, it is too late to go back and re-teach any important concepts missed or misunderstood. Thus, learners often walk away without meeting learning objectives and having wasted their time.

Section 4: Transfer of Learning

In this section, you will find games and activities that help with the all-important transfer of learning issue that so many trainers, educators, and meeting facilitators struggle with. It provides useful ways to help learners attain an "ah ha" moment in which they see how the content learned during the session will be applicable and can be applied to their own workplaces and life situations.

Section 5: Ending on a High Note

Research has shown that people best remember what they hear first and last, so it makes sense to ensure that you end your programs in a profound manner. This section provides a variety of ways to review program content and close out a session in a memorable way so that participants walk out with a better understanding of what they learned.

Resources

This section lists organizations, websites, books, music, and much more that can be used to enhance your learning experiences.

Getting the Most from This Book

As mentioned earlier, this book is designed to be a quick reference source. You can get the most from it by orienting yourself to the content and learning how and why the various content is important to successful learning events. Once you have finished reading this Introduction, scan through the contents to find games and activities that fit your specific needs. If you review each chapter thoroughly, you will likely find alternative ways of getting a point across to your learners using fun and interactive means.

Once you have read this book, you will be able to:

- Identify creative ways in which you can engage learners so that they have maximum gain from their learning experience

- Find resources that will aid you in setting a stimulating learning environment in which your learners will be more inspired, motivated, and enthusiastic about the learning that they experience

S E C T I O N 1

Getting Started

"We do not stop playing because we grow old. We grow old because we stop playing."

—Anonymous

Overview

The activities and games that you will find in this section are designed to help you start your learning events on a high note, get things moving related to your program or class content, or have people introduce themselves in fun and interesting ways.

Games and Activities in This Section

Before you can share information or teach anything to your learners, you must first capture their attention. In the *implementation* phase of the traditional instructional design model known as ADDIE (assessment, design, development, implementation, and evaluation), this element is often referred to as the "gain attention" portion of the program under the "introduction" section of a training program, class, or presentation. Typically, you will want to do something during this phase that grabs and briefly holds the attention of learners so that you can share learning objectives and the purpose of your program. Often, this can be a short personal story related to the topic, a startling statement or fact, a topic-related joke, or some other creative way of tuning learners in to the topic. It can also be done in some fun, innovative manner using activities that engage and energize a group while allowing them to get to know one another. This chapter will share ideas for creatively opening any session. There are also tips for modifying each activity to allow them to serve as energizers or for other functions. You can reduce the suggested time required for many of the activities when you have smaller numbers of learners.

1. Changing Paradigms

Time Required	Approximately 25 minutes
Purpose	This activity can be used to introduce virtually any topic by getting learners to see that preconceived ideas sometimes get in the way of successful completion of a project, attainment of a goal, or acquisition of new knowledge or skills.
Objective(s)	Through the use of magic and novelty, the facilitator will be able to:

- Introduce concepts related to a session topic;

- Engage learner brains by challenging them to think about how the trick works; and

- Deliver ideas in a creative manner.

Group Size	Up to thirty, depending on room and seating configuration (all learners must have a clear view of the facilitator) and option chosen.
Process	Have one inflated balloon and two deflated backups, the needle, and magic wand ready.

By using a little "magic," you can sometimes show learners that perhaps there are things that you have to say that are worth listening to as you tie into session topic concepts.

Pick up the inflated balloon and magic wand. Wave the wand above the balloon as you say something like, "First let me turn this ordinary balloon into a magic balloon with the wave of a wand."

Following this, put the wand down and pick up the needle, and put the tip near the inflated balloon as you ask, "How many of you know what happens when you put a sharp object, like this needle, into contact with an inflated balloon?" Many people will put their hands to their ears and will say "pop." Agree that they are probably right and then pop the balloon.

Say, "I guess your beliefs are correct."

Explain that there are many learners who have preconceived ideas similar to their belief about balloons that can hinder their ability to accept or obtain information.

Ask, "What if I can prove to you that your beliefs about the needle and balloon are incorrect? Would you be interested in hearing about other things I might be able to share with you?"

Without letting learners see you, dip the tip of the needle in the petroleum jelly (or insert it into the magic wand that contains petroleum jelly if using such a wand).

Blow up and tie the end of a second balloon and, as you deliver the following dialog, start working the needle through the balloon from the base (tied end). To do this, place the sharp tip against the rubber near the tied-off portion (where is it thickest and least stretched) and slowly start rolling or rotating the needle back and forth between your forefinger and thumb while applying a small amount of pressure to force it through the balloon. Once it is through one side of the balloon, push it through and continue rolling the needle until the point punctures and exits the top portion of the balloon.

Take it easy to prevent the balloon from popping. If it does, laugh and say, "I guess you were right about what happens when sharp objects contact inflated balloons," then blow up another balloon and continue without stopping.

Continue your dialog as you force the needle through the balloon by saying something like, "Many times preconceived ideas come from previous training or life experiences that cause learners to think that they have the answer or know what you are talking about before you say it. These preconceived ideas are known as 'paradigms.'"

Tie in a session concept that is related to a standard paradigm (for example, in a class on change management you might talk about how people sometimes believe that "We've always done it like that" is the way something has to be).

Explain that to dispel such ideas you sometimes will have to be willing to open your mind to other possibilities and not go through life limiting the way you think about or do things.

Hold the punctured balloon up with the needle still through it from both sides and say, "Just like this balloon activity demonstrates, things are not always black or white; often there is a lot of gray area if you just look for it."

To show that it is not a trick balloon, pull the needle out and pop the balloon.

Form equal-sized groups.

Have learners spend 10 minutes discussing what session-topic-related concepts they could teach in the workplace with such a needle-through-the-balloon technique.

Process Follow-Up   Take a minute to explain how the trick works so learners will not be distracted trying to figure it out and can then focus on what you are saying next. Tell learners that this is an excellent way to show others who train, educate, present, or speak or are sharing information with others, when their goal is to get people to think outside the box, to be creative and use various techniques to present ideas and teach skills (magic, games, activities, or props).

Ask: "What thoughts do you have as a result of this activity?"

"What concepts that might be taught with this technique did your group come up with?"

Option   If time permits, form small groups, give learners needles and balloons and allow them to practice the technique, then think of one topic they could use it to teach if they were the facilitator.

Props/Tools Needed

- 18-inch needle through the balloon, or a sharpened metal knitting needle (enough for all groups, if the optional format is used);

- (Optional) Magic wand (special magic wands that have a hollow center and contain petroleum jelly);

- Petroleum jelly (if not using a wand that contains it); and

- Different colored balloons.

Possible Topic Application   Unlimited

Why It Is Brain-Based   Engages on a visual, kinesthetic (optional activity), and auditory level;

Uses magic (novelty) to grab and hold attention;

Adds fun;

Uses color (balloons), which can stimulate the brain; and

Stimulates the brain (as learners try to figure how you did it).

2. Silent Engagement

Time Required   Approximately 20 minutes

Purpose   To provide a creative approach for grabbing the attention of a team or group and to involve them early in a session.

Objective(s)   Through a humorous introductory approach, the facilitator will be able to:

- Help group members get to know others in the room;

- Encourage participation; and

- Generate a level of curiosity that can later be satisfied during the activity debriefing.

Group Size   Up to thirty

Process   Prior to the session starting, create slides, transparencies, or flip-chart pages with the following questions on them. The appropriate media format will be determined by the size of the group. Color and humorous graphic images or borders should be used to enhance the text and to add a bit more levity while attracting attention.

- What is your name?

- Why are you here?

- What one thing do you most want to learn today?

- What are you thinking at this point?

When the time to start the session comes, either have someone else introduce you while you enter from behind learners, or enter from behind them using some form of noise or attention-getter (train whistle, coach's whistle, bike horn, hand clappers, or whatever to draw attention to yourself). You should also be wearing some outlandish prop (for example, a Groucho Marx nose and glasses, rubber animal nose, Cheese Head top hat and bow tie, or trick nail through the head).

Do not say a word as you proceed to the front of the room, smile, wave, and turn on the projector or turn to the flip chart to display the first prepared question.

Turn, smile, and gesture to someone in the front row and then motion to the question on the slide, transparency, or flip chart to indicate the question they should answer (e.g., What is your name?).

Randomly select four or five other learners, one at a time, and have them introduce themselves in the same fashion, all the while smiling and remaining silent.

Present the second, then third question until 3 to 5 minutes have passed, at which time you should project the final question (What are you thinking right now?) and with open arms gesture to the entire group to indicate that anyone should respond.

Typically at this point, someone will say something like, "This is different" or "This is strange." They might also ask, "Are you ever going to speak?"

Remove your prop(s) and respond, "I was wondering if you wanted me to talk." (If the question is not asked, remove the glasses, introduce yourself, explain that, while you do not take yourself seriously, you do take the topic so [stress the importance of the topic over yourself] and debrief the activity).

If the question is asked, introduce yourself and then review the activity as indicated under Process Follow-Up.

Following the process follow-up, have all learners turn to those around them and introduce themselves if they do not already know one another.

Process Follow-Up   Spend 10 minutes reviewing the outcomes of the activity.

Ask: "What was I just able to accomplish through this activity without ever saying a word?"

"How can you likewise use silence, gestures, and other nonverbal communication to effectively interact with . . ." (customers, co-workers, peers, friends/relatives, etc.)?

If the following points do not come out, point out:

- You introduced fun, humor, and a lighthearted approach to the learning environment;

- You created an atmosphere of expectation and piqued their interest;

- Without saying a word, you gained their attention;

- You intrigued and interested them;

- You got active involvement;

- You gained information about your learners that could be useful later in the program;

- You discovered which learners potentially might become actively involved and which ones might be reluctant (through the use of the open-ended questions in which you invited the entire group to give input); and

- You tied into key program concepts.

Ask: "How might some of these outcomes be applied on the job or in other environments?" (for example, to gain answers to work or session-related topics in training or in a meeting)

You may want to give small toys or candy as rewards for those who answer questions or otherwise participate during the activity.

Option(s)
1. Instead of using the activity as an opener, use it as a review following lunch or a break in which the questions are based on session content to that point.

2. The activity might be used in a team meeting or training session on virtually any topic by changing the questions in order to add a bit of novelty and get people thinking before actually beginning a presentation or meeting.

Props/Tools Needed
- Flip chart, slides, or transparencies;

- Assortment of colored markers (not needed if using slides);

- Projector and screen (not needed if using a flip chart);

- Groucho Marx nose and glasses, animal nose, or other similar prop;

- Noisemaker (whistle, bell, or clapper); and

- Small prizes or candy.

Possible Topic Application   Any session in which interpersonal communication plays a part.

Why It Is Brain-Based Engages visual and auditory learners;

Involves use of novelty to gain and hold attention;

Introduces humor and fun;

Gives learners an opportunity to become actively involved;

Causes learners to think outside the box by getting them to think of ways in which they might apply the activity to other environments; and

Involves learners.

3. Sweet Anagrams

Time Required	Approximately 30 to 35 minutes
Purpose	To provide a fun approach for getting a team or group into the mindset for problem solving.
Objective(s)	Through a lighthearted activity, the facilitator will be able to:

- Help learners get to know one another and stimulate communication;

- Encourage active participation;

- Generate a high level of energy; and

- Prompt learners to start thinking about problem solving.

Group Size	Up to thirty
Process	Create a slide, transparency, or flip chart (depending on Group Size and resources) that has the anagrams shown at the end of this activity on it.

Form learners into equal-sized groups (see Creatively Forming Groups in the Introduction).

Have a leader designated for each group (see Creatively Selecting Volunteers in the Introduction). Explain that their role is to monitor time and assist the group throughout the process.

Explain that people sometimes need a "nudge" to get started with creative problem solving.

Display the list of anagrams.

Tell learners that each of the anagrams is the scrambled name of something they probably see regularly.

Explain that they will have 15 minutes to try to solve all the anagrams.

Say that when any group leader thinks his or her group has all the correct answers, the leader shouts out, "We have it!"

Verify responses and, if correct, proclaim that group as the winner. If they have incorrect responses, tell everyone to continue until time is up.

After 15 minutes, use some form of noisemaker (bell, whistle, horn, music, or other loud device) to signal time is up.

Show a slide, transparency, or flip-chart page with the correct responses, if desired.

Reward the winning team members with all the correct answers with incentives (for example, First Place ribbons, candy, small toys, or whatever). If no team found all the responses in time, reward the team with the most correct answers.

Reward all group leaders for "volunteering" and stress that with active involvement comes reward throughout the session (assuming you plan to use incentives during your session).

Process Follow-Up   *Ask:* "What process did your team use to come up with the correct responses?"

"What did and did not work?"

"What role did communication play in the process of solving the anagrams?"

"What role did the leaders play in the process? How does this relate to your experience in the workplace?"

"How can your approach(es) used in this activity be applied in the workplace?"

Explain that by harnessing the brain power of many people in a group, better ideas and solutions can often be gained, thereby potentially saving time, effort, and money and reducing errors.

Option(s)   1. Use as an individual activity to energize learners following a break or lunch or a period of tedious work or study to give them a mental break and lighten the atmosphere;

2. Use as an interim or final review activity by creating anagrams from key words or concepts used in a session; and

3. Customize the activity by selecting your own terms (from your session, industry, company, product/service line, etc.) and create your own anagrams (see Resources for a free online anagram site that scrambles words for you).

Props/Tools Needed	• Anagram slide and solution slide or transparencies (if used);
	• Laptop PC with PowerPoint® (if used);
	• LCD or overhead projector and screen (if used);
	• Flip chart with pad (if using one or not using slides or transparencies); and
	• Rewards for teams and leaders.
Possible Topic Application	Any session in which problem solving, interpersonal communication, and team building are important.
Why It Is Brain-Based	Engages learners' visual, auditory, and kinesthetic learning styles;
	Adds fun to the session;
	Actively involves learners;
	Adds an element of eustress (good stress) through competition;
	Stimulates interaction and communication (if doing as a team activity); and
	Provides a vehicle for introducing, reinforcing, or reviewing content, which aids memory and learning.

Creative Learning: Activities and Games That REALLY Engage People. Copyright © 2007 by Robert W. Lucas.
Reprinted by permission of Pfeiffer, an Imprint of Wiley. www.pfeiffer.com

Candy Types and Anagrams Solutions

Milky Way	yawilk my
Snickers	cress kin
Hershey Kisses	sees hers hi skys
Butterfinger	be return gift
Nestle Crunch	clenches turn
Almond Joy	joan old my
Junior Mints	i jim son runt
Milk Duds	mild dusk
Raisinets	a sinister
Sno Caps	cap sons
Sugar Babies	sara be big us
Whoppers	perp show

4. Fantasyland

Time Required	45 minutes
Purpose	To encourage learners to think of ways that they might immediately apply session content to their workplace.
Objective(s)	To provide a vehicle through which learners can:

- Identify key issues facing them in the workplace; and

- Develop a list of possible things that they need to address in their workplace or life.

Group Size	Thirty
Process	Form equal-sized groups of five or six learners (see Creatively Forming Groups in the Introduction).

Randomly select a leader (speaker, facilitator, and timekeeper) and scribe (note-taker) for each group (see Creatively Selecting Volunteers in the Introduction).

Have everyone close their eyes and relax.

Turn on easy-listening instrumental music (see Suggested Music/ Visualization/Relaxation in the Resource section).

Tell learners that they have magically been transported to Fantasyland, where anything in the workplace is possible. For example, they can change anything they dislike in their workplace (boss, customers, peers, job tasks, or the environment), they can add things to enhance their current environment, and they can modify their job tasks or customers.

Encourage them to think of *positive* workplace or other situations they have experienced and the qualities that made them so.

After 3 minutes, have everyone open their eyes and jot down elements of their ideal positive workplace environments (for example, a boss who listens and really cares about employees) on a piece of paper, number them in order of what they believe to be importance, then share their top items with team members.

As learners share their key elements, the group scribe should capture a list of the top items shared by each person. Then the group should identify any that were similar. If none were alike, have group members select the one item that is most common among all of their environments.

Have each group spend 10 minutes discussing how their organization already makes or would make the key element identified by their group a reality. You may want to have a scribe capture the ideas on a flip-chart page for later use.

Next, randomly ask group leaders to spend no more than 3 minutes sharing the key element of an ideal workplace that their group identified and how it might become a reality in organizations with the rest of the groups.

After all groups have reported, suggest that, based on what they just heard, they now have a checklist of what makes an ideal workplace in the minds of many people and that they might want to strive to change their own workplace to mirror this fantasy environment.

Reward group leaders and scribes.

Have everyone give a round of applause for their great ideas.

Later in the program, you may want to revisit the lists from this activity and have groups create action plans for making changes. This will give them a tangible result that they can take back to their workplaces and adds value to the training.

Process Follow-Up   *Ask:* "What ideas did you think of or hear that might realistically be applied in your own workplace?"

"Who can you enlist to help you make some of these changes a reality?"

"What would need to be done to make some of the changes you've thought or heard about?"

Option(s)   1. To shorten this activity by approximately 20 minutes, you can make this purely an individual activity, which eliminates the needs for group discussion and voting;

2. You can modify the topic that learners address in this activity to focus on any issue you desire that relates specifically to your program topic; or

3. The activity can be used as a discussion starter when change is proposed or occurring in organizations.

Props/Tools Needed
- Paper;

- Pencils;

- CD player; and

- Easy-listening music (see Suggested Music in the Resource section).

Possible Topic Application   Any session in which change is an element of desired outcomes.

Why It Is Brain-Based   Involves use of music and mental visioning;

Engages learners on a visual and auditory level;

Ties into several of the eight of Gardner's multiple intelligences (interpersonal, intrapersonal, and linguistic);

Brings learners together to exchange and discuss ideas; and

Uses rewards/incentives to potentially help motivate and involve learners.

5. I Can Identify with That

Time Required	45 minutes
Purpose	To provide a humorous means of having people introduce themselves and to identify characteristics, strengths, knowledge, or skills possessed.
Objective(s)	Through use of common items, the facilitator will be able to:

- Provide a means of introduction and information sharing by learners or group attendees;

- Create a non-threatening environment conducive to communication; and

- Potentially identify people who are better communicators, quicker thinkers, or more open to sharing if these traits will be useful later in the program.

Group Size	Twenty-five
Process	Use this activity at the beginning of a session.

Put a variety of items of similar types (common household utensils, toys, articles of clothing, assortment of fruits or vegetables) in the center of each table and tell participants to select one that they prefer.

Give them 2 minutes to "get to know their item."

At the end of 2 minutes, have learners in turn introduce themselves and then describe one feature or aspect of the selected item that is "just like them" and represents a characteristic, strength, knowledge, or skill they have that will help them be successful at whatever knowledge or skill set the program they are attending addresses. For example, in a program on customer service, someone might say he is personable and gets along well with others.

Note	Start this off by selecting an item and introducing yourself in the manner described to provide an example of what is expected.

After all learners have done a self-introduction, have them give a round of applause in unison to celebrate their willingness to share and their new knowledge of what they can appreciate in one another.

Process Follow-Up   *Ask:* "How might this activity process be used in other environments (for example, team meetings)?"

Option   At the beginning of a session, form groups of three to four participants (see Creatively Forming Groups in the Introduction); randomly select a group spokesperson (see Creatively Selecting "Volunteers" in the Introduction);

Have each group select one item from the pile on the table;

Tell them they have 5 to 10 minutes to get to know their items intimately—size, shape, weight, features, texture, or whatever else applies—and to identify one aspect of the item that relates to all group members. For example, if you were conducting a session on change management using toys and someone picked up an eight-inch foam die, all members of the group might identify that a die is usually associated with the game of chance. They might all then agree that, from a change perspective, they are all willing to take a chance that the new process, policy, procedure, or whatever being implemented in their organization will work;

At the end of 10 minutes, have participants introduce themselves to the others in the room by sharing who they are and what they do for a living, or as an alternative, who they are and something that others do not generally know about them;

Have the group spokespersons introduce themselves last;

The spokesperson is to then describe the one common feature or aspect of the group's selected item that is "just like them" and represents a characteristic, strength, knowledge, or skill all group members share and that will help them be successful at whatever knowledge or skill set the program they are attending addresses;

After all spokespersons have done this, have everyone give a round of applause for their insights, creativity, and willingness to "share intimate details" about themselves (do this in a humorous fashion);

Reward spokespersons with a small prize related to the program topic or give candy.

Props/Tools Needed
- Assortment of items so that each person will have something and a few items will be left over (to allow choice); and

- Small prizes or candy.

Possible Topic Applications   Any session in which group interaction, interpersonal communication, and team building are desired outcomes.

Why It Is Brain-Based   Engages visual, auditory, and kinesthetic learners;

Gets learners actively involved and communicating;

Creates an open environment for sharing;

Involves movement;

Adds novelty and humor;

Stimulates both the left and right brain through language and creativity; and

Involves use of recognition, incentives, or rewards.

6. High Card

Time Required   10 to 15 minutes

Purpose   To provide a fun way to allow for individual introductions in classes, training sessions, or meetings where people either do not know one another or do not know one another well.

Objective(s)   Through a short icebreaker activity, the facilitator will provide a means for learners or group members to:

- Get to know one another;

- Learn facts about their peers that they possibly did not know; and

- Create an atmosphere of openness that can later assist during meaningful program topic discussions.

Group Size   Unlimited

Process   Prior to your learners' arrival, gather enough card decks so that each person will receive one card. Select only the cards numbered 1 through 3 from each of the four suits per deck. Using higher-numbered cards will bog the process down as people try to think of things to say.

As each person arrives, greet him or her and have the person pick a card randomly from a deck without looking at it.

As an alternative, you can randomly place one card on each learner's seat (face down) so that they can retrieve them as they arrive.

Tell learners that they should stand up, in turn, do a brief introduction by sharing names, what they do, and a number of non-work-related things about themselves that others would not know. The number of items they should disclose is based on the numbers on their cards (have them display the card to the group as they begin).

Ask for a volunteer to begin the introductions.

Reward this person with candy or small prize and tell the group that "with effort and initiative comes reward" throughout this session.

Tell the group that the volunteer will start the process by introducing him- or herself and then the introductions will proceed left or right (as you designate).

Explain that information they provide can be related to hobbies, family, favorite memories, education, vacations, favorite books, or whatever they choose.

Process Follow-Up At the end of the activity ask:

- "What did you hear about your fellow attendees that you are surprised or impressed by?"

- "How many of you heard something identified that you share and that might form the basis for a discussion with someone later (shared hobby or interest)?"

Option(s)

1. Instead of cards, you can create colorful strips of paper with the numbers on them;

2. Instead of individual introductions, create equal-sized small groups and allow small group introductions. If time permits and the concept of sharing and getting to know one another better is important, you might have everyone rotate to different tables to form new groups and repeat the activity. This will take a bit of planning and designating each attendee by a number, color, or some other means before or at the beginning of the session to ensure that when rotation occurs people do not end up sitting with people they already met in the first round;

3. Use the activity as an energizer sometime during the day, without introductions, rather than at the beginning of a session or meeting. This will provide a means of having people get to know one another better.

Props/Tools Needed

- Playing card decks or colored paper strips with numbers; and

- Prizes or candy.

Possible Topic Application Any topic or meeting where introductions are needed or where you want people to share information about themselves in order to improve communication.

Why It Is Brain-Based Fun;

Novel;

Stimulates learners from a visual, auditory, and kinesthetic perspective; and

Helps create a non-threatening environment.

7. What Were You Doing?

Time Required	30 minutes
Purpose	To provide learners with an opportunity to get to know one another and to share a bit of information about themselves with others.
Objective(s)	Through a non-threatening, fun activity, the facilitator will provide a means for learners or group members to:

- Start the session off in a positive manner;

- Get to know one another;

- Learn facts about their peers that they possibly did not know; and

- Create an atmosphere of openness that can later lead to meaningful program topic discussions.

Group Size	Twenty-five
Process	Prior to the start of a session, collect twenty-six coins with a variety of dates that are no older than ten years prior to the start date of your session.

At the beginning of the activity, pass out one coin to each learner.

Explain that each person is to introduce him- or herself and tell what his or her function is in the workplace (or elsewhere if the session is not being held in a workplace).

Tell learners that they are also to tell something about their lives in the year that their coins were minted (attending college, working at. . ., having a baby, etc.).

Start the activity by introducing yourself and telling something that was happening in your life, based on a coin you chose.

Process Follow-Up	*Ask:* "What did you learn about another learner that you thought was interesting, that you did not know before, or that was surprising to you?"

Encourage learners to network during break/lunch with someone who told something that is of interest or that is a shared interest.

Explain that, by knowing more about one another, the workplace can be more effective because personal strengths and areas of preference can be drawn upon and relationships can grow.

Option(s)

1. Use as an energizer activity to increase communication during a session;

2. Have learners select a life event that prepared them for the session topic (for example, if they are attending a class on problem solving, they might choose a prior life experience that will aid them in problem solving); or

3. Use in a train-the-trainer session in which learners can share something about themselves that will enable them to become a better trainer (for example, someone might reveal that she took a course on effective listening in college and that will aid her as a trainer or educator).

Props/Tools Needed

Twenty-six coins dated within the past ten years.

Possible Topic Application

Any session in which desired outcomes include networking, enhanced interpersonal communication, or teamwork.

Why It Is Brain-Based

Adds fun to a session;

Incorporates novelty;

Causes people to reflect on previous life experiences (accessing memory); and

Non-threatening.

8. Meeting Nose to Nose

Time Required	45 minutes
Purpose	To provide a means to allow learners to get to know one another and to share their goals for the session.
Objective(s)	In a humorous and novel manner, the facilitator will help learners to:

- Become acquainted with one another;
- Share information about themselves with others; and
- Discuss the learning goals.

Group Size	Up to forty-eight
Process	Purchase enough rubber animal noses so that each learner will have one and that there are an equal number of each type, based on group size.

Prepare small paper bags by writing "Do not open until told" with a colored marker, placing one nose in each bag, then stapling the bags closed.

Either place bags in a pile in the center of learner tables or give each person a bag as he or she enters the room.

When you are ready to start the activity, tell everyone to open their paper bags, reach in, take out what they find, and then put the item on for the duration of the activity.

Explain that learners are to stand up and find others who are wearing the same type of nose or those who "look like" them and form small groups with these people.

Select a group leader (spokesperson, facilitator, and timekeeper) and scribe (note-taker) for each group (see Creatively Selecting Volunteers in the Introduction).

Give each group a sheet of flip-chart paper and a variety of colored markers.

Tell learners that they have 20 minutes to introduce themselves to their peers and then brainstorm a list of things they want to gain from the session.

When time has elapsed, sound a noisemaker (whistle, bell, or gong) to regain attention.

Process Follow-Up	Have scribes post their groups' lists on the wall for viewing by everyone.
	In turn, have group leaders present their groups' lists to the rest of the groups.
	If appropriate, add any of the items identified to the program objectives list.
	Once all group lists have been presented, have everyone give a round of applause for their great ideas and effort.
	Reward group leaders and scribes with candy or small prizes (toys related to the program topic).
Option(s)	1. Instead of passing out individual bags, get bags large enough to hold up to eight noses (depending on group size). Place noses in bags, staple them shut and place them in the center of round learner tables. When you are ready to start the activity, have someone at each table open the bag on that table, reach in, and select an item without looking and then put it on to wear for the duration the activity. Have other learners at each table do likewise until everyone is wearing an animal nose. Continue with the rest of activity as in the Process section.
	2. Use the format described in the original activity above but discuss key session concepts after forming groups.
Props/Tools Needed	• Assorted rubber animal noses;
	• Paper bags;
	• Assorted colored markers;
	• Flip-chart paper;
	• Masking tape; and
	• Candy or small prizes.
Possible Topic Application	Any session with a desired outcome of networking, interpersonal communication, or team building.
Why It Is Brain-Based	Involves use of humor, fun, and novelty;
	Engages learners in group activity;
	Causes physical movement;

Involves visual, auditory, and kinesthetic learning;

Causes learners to reflect and generate ideas;

Uses color (markers and noses); and

Potentially stimulates learning.

9. Scavenger Hunt

Time Required	25 minutes
Purpose	To create an opportunity for learners to become actively involved at the beginning of a learning event.
Objective(s)	By hiding program content around the room, the facilitator will be able to:

- Start learners thinking about session concepts before the presentation of content actually begins;

- Generate friendly competition between learners; and

- Provide a novel way for learners to introduce themselves.

Group Size	Twenty-five
Process	Prior to learners arriving for a session, create a series of session-topic-related tips written on 2-by-3-inch colored strips and post these tips in various places around the room (under chairs, under saucers of a coffee cup, taped to the side or back of a flip-chart easel, at the bottom of a poster or chart posted on the wall). You may want to make a list of where you hide these to ensure all are found. When creating the strips, make a few duplicates to throw learners off and require them to search a bit longer.

As part of your opening introduction, tell learners that "Before you introduce yourself and we start, we're going to go on a little scavenger hunt for some tips about the content of today's session."

When ready, tell learners that they have 5 minutes to locate a list of [*number*] tips on 2-by-3-inch colored paper strips that you have posted in various places around the room.

Tell them to write down the tips they find on a sheet of paper and leave the strip where it is for others to find.

Explain that the first person getting all [*number*] of different tips should call out "Finished" and, if he or she has them all, he or she will receive a prize.

Tell them that there are some duplicates hidden.

Make sure that each learner has a pencil/pen and sheet of blank paper.

Shout "Go," turn on some upbeat music (Mexican hat dance or other selection from the Suggested Music listing in the Resource section) and watch the fun as learners scurry to find the tips.

At the end of 5 minutes or when someone has all the tips, sound a noisemaker and ask learners to have a seat.

Reward the winner with a small prize or toy related to the session topic.

Starting with the winner and proceeding to the person's right or left, have each person introduce him- or herself and share one tip he or she found. Do this until all tips have been exhausted, at which point learners should just introduce themselves.

Give everyone a piece of candy (to replace the brain cells and calories they burned up!).

Process Follow-Up   Show a slide or flip chart with all tips listed so that everyone can compare their listings;

Go through each of the tips and ask why learners think it might be helpful; and

Have everyone give a round of applause for their efforts.

Option(s)   1. Instead of tips, use the strips to introduce actual points from your presentation content (depending on the session topic, this could be something like the five most important things to remember about delivering quality service, Gardner's eight multiple intelligences, or Kirkpatrick's four levels of evaluation);

2. Use the activity as either an interim or final review; or

3. Instead of tips or key session points, put numbers on the strips of paper.

   Explain that [*total number*] of numbered strips have been hidden around the room and that in a minute they will have an opportunity to search for them.

   Tell them that as soon as they find one strip to bring it to you.

   When ready to begin, turn on some upbeat music (an Irish Jig or a selection from the Suggested Music listing in the Resources section).

   Have learners search for the strips.

When you receive a numbered strip, hand the person giving it to you a 3-by-5 card with a corresponding number (same as on the strip) and one key session concept on it and have the person sit down.

After all learners have either received a strip or all strips have been recovered (depending on how many there were) have everyone sit down.

In turn, have each person who has a 3-by-5 card read his or her concept and define it. Reward those who successfully define the concept with a small prize or candy. If someone does not know what the concept means, ask for a volunteer to explain it and reward that learner.

After all concepts have been reviewed, have everyone give a round of applause for their efforts.

Give everyone a piece of candy (to replace the brain cells and calories they burned up!

Props/Tools Needed
- 2-by-3-inch colored strips of paper with tips on them posted around the room;
- 3-by-5 index cards (if using option 3);
- Masking tape;
- Pen/pencil for each learner;
- Blank paper;
- Music and boom box; and
- Small prizes.

Possible Topic Application
Any session in which group interaction, team building, networking, and interpersonal communication are desired outcomes.

Why It Is Brain-Based
Adds fun;

Generates excitement and stimulates the brain;

Physically and mentally engages learners;

Uses color;

Adds music or sound to the environment;

Incorporates rewards; and

Causes reflection and memory recall (option 2).

10. Making the Rules

Time Required   10 minutes

Purpose   To allow learners an opportunity to generate a list of session or meeting "rules" that will make the event more productive.

Objective(s)   Through the use of a group activity, the facilitator will be able to:

- Involve learners early in a session;

- Capture learner thoughts related to how an ideal learning event or meeting should progress; and

- Provide guidelines for order and procedure that will be used during an event.

Group Size   Twenty-five

Process   Prior to learners or attendees arriving, create a flip-chart page (you may need several depending on the number of guidelines developed) titled SESSION GUIDELINES.

Cut additional sheets of flip-chart paper horizontally into 3-inch-high strips so that there are enough strips for each learner to have one.

At the beginning of the learning event or meeting, introduce yourself and give opening comments. Explain that for any event to run smoothly and be productive, guidelines are helpful.

Hand out the 3-inch-wide strips of paper and masking tape.

Give out various colored markers.

Tell learners that they should print one idea they have on acceptable behavior in a learning event (meeting) on a strip. Suggest that they use short phrases rather than long sentences. Encourage them to add clever graphics if they like. If necessary, have them put a piece of blank paper under their strips as they write with the marker so that the ink does not come through onto tablecloths or furniture.

After everyone has written down their thoughts, ask for a volunteer to introduce him- or herself, then come forward and tape his or her idea to the flip-chart page you created earlier.

Reward the volunteer with candy or a small prize.

In turn, have all other learners do likewise.

If there are duplicates of something already posted, a learner does not need to come forward, just state that the idea is already posted and introduce him- or herself.

Add any additional important guidelines that the group may have missed. Suggested guidelines include:

- Turn off all electronic devices;

- Get permission before speaking;

- Respect the views of others;

- Refrain from interrupting others;

- No side conversations with others—direct all comments to the facilitator or group;

- Get involved in the learning process;

- Return from breaks on time; and

- Clean up after yourself.

Process Follow-Up After all learners have posted their suggested guidelines, explain that these are the guidelines that will be followed during the session (meeting).

Option(s) Instead of session guidelines, you can have learners create a list of session-specific issues or answer a question that you have posted on a flip-chart page, slide, or writing surface. For example:

- "What one thing do you most want to learn today?"

- "What do you hope does NOT happen in today's session (meeting)?"

- "What one thing can you do to personally contribute to the success of today's session (meeting)?"

- "What concerns do you have related to today's session (meeting)?"

Props/Tools Needed	• Flip-chart paper;
	• Easel;
	• Scissors;
	• Masking tape;
	• Various colored markers; and
	• Candy or small prizes.

Possible Topic Application   Unlimited

Why It Is Brain-Based   Engages learners mentally and physically;

Involves everyone in the learning process;

Appeals to visual, auditory, and kinesthetic learners;

Adds color with the markers, which stimulates the brain; and

Uses rewards, which can stimulate involvement and potentially motivate learners.

11. Characteristic Card Swap

Time Required	45 minutes
Purpose	To energize learners at the beginning of a session, generate discussion, and aid introductions.
Objective(s)	Through the use of a small group activity, the facilitator will be able to:

- Prompt introductions among learners;

- Encourage the exchange of information; and

- Gain insights into how learners view themselves.

Group Size	Twenty-four
Process	Prior to the session beginning, create a deck of cards with the terms shown on the list of characteristics at the end of this activity using 3-by-5 index cards.

Create flip-chart pages with the first name of each person (use last initials too if there is more than one person sharing a name) listed vertically down the left side of the page(s). Leave enough space so that each person can tape a 3-by-5 card next to his or her name. Tape these pages to the wall somewhere near the front of the room or wherever they are most visible.

Additionally, have a spare empty table somewhere in the room for displaying extra cards during the activity.

When ready to start the activity, have each learner pick four cards from the deck.

Explain that they are to assemble in the rear of the room and spend 15 minutes introducing themselves to one another as they compare cards.

Their goal is to keep four cards at all times, while obtaining the four cards that they feel most accurately identify characteristics about themselves.

They can swap cards as many times as they like until they have four cards that they feel most closely describe their own characteristics. For example, if two learners meet and one has a card needed by the other person, they can swap one card, then move to other learners in search of more cards to complete their sets.

Give a 2-minute warning before time is up.

At the end of 15 minutes, sound a noisemaker to regain attention.

Ask: "Who does not feel that he or she has cards that adequately describe him or her?"

Say: "Like many organizations that experience change, the rules for this activity have changed. You now have 3 minutes to review the additional cards on the table (point to them), and you may exchange any of your cards for ones that more closely describe your own personal characteristics."

After 3 minutes, have everyone sit down.

Say: "Once again the rules have changed for the activity. You have 1 minute to select the one card (from the four that you have) that best describes you."

At the end of 1 minute sound a noisemaker.

Ask for a volunteer to introduce him- or herself and to share what one characteristic best describes him or her and why that is true.

Once the volunteer has finished, have the person tape his or her card next to his or her name on the posted flip-chart pages containing learner names.

Reward the volunteer with candy or a small prize.

Have all learners in turn introduce themselves and place their cards on the flip-cart page(s).

After everyone has finished, you may want to introduce yourself and share what characteristic best describes you so that learners feel a bit more comfortable about you.

Process Follow-Up Explain that knowing one another better can aid communication during the session.

Ask: "How can knowing information about co-workers, such as that shared in this activity, aid you in your workplace?"

"What did you learn about yourself as you had to whittle down your card selections to only one term?"

"How did you feel when you had to let go of the characteristics and define yourself with just one?"

"How do you feel about the one term you ultimately kept?"

Possible answers: Can help build and strengthen relationships and form stronger teams;

Allows you to tap into peer strengths for projects; or

Allows you to share your strengths to help others in areas in which they may not be strong.

Have everyone give a round of applause for their efforts.

Option(s)

1. Create four card sets and place each in a separate large manila envelope. Form four equal-sized teams and have learners work in their teams.

   Follow the process outlined above except that they may go back to remaining cards in their envelopes to trade cards after their original selection, rather than going to one large table area. This will help to cut down on chaos if you have a large group.

2. Instead of doing the activity as an opening icebreaker, build it into session content and use it to reinforce issues such as team support and understanding, acceptance of others, versatility, diversity, or other topic related to people skills.

Props/Tools Needed

- Flip-chart paper;
- Flip-chart easel;
- Various colored markers;
- Masking tape;
- Extra table;
- 3-by-5 multi-colored index cards; and
- Candy or small prizes.

Possible Topic Application

This activity can be used as an energizer during sessions dealing with relationship building, team building, interpersonal communication, customer service, and orientation. It can help to bring out issues related to the need for effective communication, team building, and consensus building that can be tied to a session topic.

Why It Is Brain-Based   Fun and novelty added to the environment;

Engages learners mentally and physically;

Involves several of Gardner's multiple intelligences;

Provides opportunity to reflect and do self-analysis;

Incorporates rewards; and

Adds additionally color to the environment, which can aid the stimulation of brain neurons.

Characteristics for Card Swap

Humble	Risk-Taker	Charming
Patient	Analytical	Daring
Admirable	Confrontational	Methodical
Persuasive	Approachable	Indirect
Generous	Insensitive	Resistant to change
Bold	Team player	Indecisive
Diplomatic	Individualistic	Thorough
Kind	Direct	Conscientious
Forceful	Inspiring	Perfectionist
Impulsive	Enthusiastic	Avoid details
Predictable	Pessimistic	Good communicator
Accurate	Optimistic	Demanding
Competitive	Disorganized	Good time manager
Sociable	Organized	Poor time manager
Deliberate	Good listener	Honest
Agreeable	Poor listener	Cooperative
Decisive	Empathetic	Avoid deadlines
Logical	Systematic	Dependable
Tactful	Focused	Avoid ambiguity
Contented	Well-disciplined	Respectful
Precise	Fearful	Controlled
Detail-oriented	Gentle	Careful
Articulate	Critical thinker	Courteous
Challenging	Popular	People-oriented
Task-oriented	Joyful	Charming

Entertaining	Friendly	Talkative
Fun-loving	Cheerful	Outspoken
Persuasive	Extroverted	Introverted
Persistent	Advent	Humorous Pioneering
Stubborn	Aggressive	Timid
Bold	Argumentative	Insistent
Problem solver	Strong-willed	Forceful
Determined	Confident	Independent
Daring	Self-assured	Practical
Helpful	Energetic	Trustworthy
Loyal	Easygoing	Conservative
Liberal	Objective	Subjective

12. Who Am I?

Time Required	25 minutes
Purpose	To provide learners with a fun opportunity to introduce themselves and get to know their peers a bit better.
Objective(s)	Through a relaxed approach to introductions, this icebreaker will allow the facilitator to:

- Engage learners early in a session;

- Reduce anxiety by allowing learners to get to know one another better; and

- Encourage learners to start communicating openly early in a session.

Group Size	Up to twenty-five
Process	When ready to start the activity, hand out blank stick-on name tags to learners.

Explain that they are to write four or five short bits of information about themselves on their nametags that should include non-visible aspects (high school or college graduate, father or mother, only/oldest/youngest/middle child, author, or pilot).

Tell them that, once they complete this task, they should turn their nametags in to you.

Once everyone has finished, place the nametags in a pile on a table and tell everyone to come up to get one (making sure not to take their own).

After everyone has a nametag, they are to spend 15 minutes searching for the person it applies to, introducing themselves, and getting to know the person a bit.

Stress that they should not become too engulfed in the introductions because someone else has their nametags and needs to meet them.

At the end of 15 minutes, sound a noisemaker to regain attention.

Determine whether there is anyone who has not found the owner of the nametag he or she selected.

If so, have those people match up for introductions and continue for 5 more minutes.

At the end of 5 minutes, sound the noisemaker and ask everyone to have a seat.

Process Follow-Up   Stress the value and importance of networking and getting to know one another since there is so much knowledge in the room.

Ask: "Was anyone surprised about what you learned from other participants? If so, by what?"

Let learners know that they will have breaks and other opportunities to get to know one another during the session (if this is applicable to your session).

Option(s)   1. Instead of having learners put characteristics or personal aspects on the nametags, have them write three or four strengths that they have related to the session topic. Then conduct the remainder of the activity as outlined above; or

2. Use as a closing activity conducted in the same way except that, instead of introduction, learners should write one thing that was covered in the session that they are confident about being able to do. When learners locate the owner of the nametags they selected, they should ask for tips on how they too can be more comfortable with the knowledge or skill identified.

Props/Tools Needed   • Nametags; and

• Noisemaker (bell, whistle, hand clapper, or gong);

Possible Topic Application   Any session in which interpersonal communication, networking, and team building are desired outcomes.

Why It Is Brain-Based   Engages learners mentally and physically;

Appeals to visual, auditory, and kinesthetic learners; and

Uses sound, which can stimulate the brain and attract attention.

SECTION 2

Re-Energizing the Brain

"If you want to be creative, stay in part a child, with the creativity and invention that characterizes children before they are deformed by adult society."

—Jean Piaget

Overview

The content of Section 2 is focused on helping raise and maintain participant energy, attentiveness, and motivation. From a learning standpoint, this is important because, for the human brain to grasp and assimilate concepts into memory, people must first be alert in order to focus on stimuli (for example, information being presented, audiovisual aids, support materials, and other crucial components of the learning environment). By providing periodic breaks from learning, you can add a spirit of fun and energy to the environment that can potentially stimulate brain neurons.

Games and Activities in This Section

13. Putting Your Memory to Work

Time Required	20 minutes
Purpose	To provide a mental break and energize learners during a session.
Objective(s)	Through the use of an activity that relies on learner memory, the facilitator will be able to:

- Provide a fun and novel means of involving learners;

- Tap learner memory to increase their level of alertness; and

- Reinforce the value of repetition in learning.

Group Size	Twenty-five
Process	Copy the slogans (but not the answers) found on the Putting Your Memory to Work Handout onto a flip-chart page with multiple colored markers prior to the session beginning (you can also use a slide or transparency).

Give each learner some sort of noisemaker (plastic hand clapper, whistle, or clicker).

Explain that learners will be participating in a fun activity during which they will be viewing slogans or marketing phrases for major products that have been advertised in recent years.

They are to indicate their knowledge of an answer by sounding their clickers.

The first person recognized will have an opportunity to respond. If the person has the wrong answer, others can sound their noisemakers and be recognized until someone guesses right.

Reward correct responses with candy or small prizes related to the session topic (for example, you could give away toys with images of money on them or dollar sign erasers in a session at a bank or credit union).

When ready to begin the activity, display the flip-charted items one at a time (by using the revelation technique of pulling the bottom of the page up to cover all but the first item and taping it to the page to prevent additional items from being viewed).

Continue until all items on the list have been correctly identified.

Process Follow-Up   Following the activity, explain that this simple exercise shows the power of repetition because the slogans or phrases are seen over and over in various forms of media when companies advertise. Tell them that you will also be using repetition in your session by introducing topics in different ways and doing reviews.

Ask: "How is this concept of repetition valuable in training or educational settings?"

"How can repetition be valuable in the workplace or other environment?"

"Does your organization use repetition effectively? If so, in what way?"

Have everyone give themselves a round of applause for their efforts.

Option(s)   1. Use as an opening icebreaker to wake learners up and show that, while the session topic is serious, the approach that you will take to it will not be boring; or

2. Use as an individual activity in which each person receives a copy of the handout and the first person with all answers correct wins a prize. This can be done at any point during a session, but works well immediately following a break or lunch as an enticement to bring people back on time.

Prior to them leaving the room for a break, explain that there will be a fun activity for them on their seats when they return and that the first person completing it correctly wins a prize.

Props/Tools Needed   • Flip-chart paper, a slide, or transparency;

• Various colored markers (if using flip-chart paper);

• Noisemakers;

• Masking tape; and

• Candy or small prizes.

Possible Topic Applications	Unlimited
Why It Is Brain-Based	Adds fun and novelty;
	Taps into previous knowledge or learning and memory;
	Recognizes and rewards behavior;
	Incorporates color;
	Appeals to visual, auditory, and kinesthetic learners; and
	Engages learners.

Putting Your Memory to Work Handout

Slogans	Answers
1. Good to the last drop	Maxwell House coffee
2. Just do it!	Nike
3. The breakfast of champions	Wheaties
4. Mmm-mmm good!	Campbell's soup
5. We do chicken right	KFC
6. Let your fingers do the walking	Yellow Pages
7. Leave the driving to us	Greyhound
8. Must-see TV	NBC
9. Because you're worth it	L'Oréal
10. Think outside the bun	Taco Bell
11. Have it your way	Burger King
12. Raising the bar	Cingular Wireless
13. We bring good things to life	GE or General Electric
14. I'm lovin' it	McDonald's
15. Can you hear me now?	Verizon

14. Sentence Sense

Time Required 25 minutes

Purpose To provide a vehicle though which learners can work together to solve a problem.

Objective(s) Through a fun small-group activity, the facilitator will be able to:

- Energize learners; and

- Provide physical and mental stimulation.

Group Size Up to twenty-four

Process Prior to the start of the learning event, create a sentence handout based on program content, similar to the sample Sentence Sense Handout at the end of this activity.

Make two copies of your Sentence Sense Handout and cut each into pieces, as indicated on the handout. Be prepared to give them out during the activity;

In addition to the handout, create a flip-chart page, slide, or transparency with the quote from the handout on it. Do not show this to learners in advance.

When ready to begin, have learners form two equal-sized groups around tables and number them group 1 and group 2.

Give out one piece of one handout to each person in group 1 and one piece from the second handout to each person in group 2. If there are twelve or fewer learners, form a single group. Some people may need to receive two handout pieces.

Explain that each of them has a word of a quote and that their goal is to determine what that quote is within 5 minutes.

Answer any questions they have and indicate that they should begin.

The first group finishing should yell out "DONE!"

Verify that they have the correct interpretation and announce either that the activity is over or that groups should continue.

If one group is successful, show the flip chart, slide, or transparency with the correct quote.

If neither group is successful within 5 minutes, sound a noisemaker, have them take a seat, and show the flip-chart page, slide, or transparency with the complete paragraph on it.

Process Follow-Up   *Ask:* "What process did you use to solve the problem?"

"How was your process successful, or not?"

"How might this process be successfully applied in the workplace?"

"What was the biggest challenge in the activity?"

"How did you overcome the challenge (if they were successful)?"

"What created barriers to your success (if they were not successful)?"

"For those who were successful, at what point did you figure out the pattern of the paragraph?"

Relate the need for teamwork to be successful in this activity to the need for teamwork in the workplace and many other life situations.

Have everyone give a round of applause for their efforts.

Reward successful team members with candy or small prizes.

Option(s)   1. Instead of creating your own handout, use the Sentence Sense Handout provided. If you do this, focus learner attention on concepts such as effectively communicating, teamwork, and problem solving that can tie to a number of session topics; or

2. Instead of using the activity as an energizer, use it as an opening ice-breaker in which you have learners form groups, introduce themselves, and then attempt to determine the quote.

Props/Tools Needed   • Handouts;

• Flip chart, slide, or transparency with solution shown;

• Noisemaker; and

• Candy or small prizes.

Possible Topic Application   Any session in which problem solving, teamwork, and interpersonal communication are desired outcomes.

Why It Is Brain-Based   Requires use of both left (verbal, logical) and right brain (spatial, visual, sees wholes);

Engages learners mentally and physically;

Involves sound (noisemaker);

Appeals to visual, auditory, and kinesthetic learners; and

Recognizes and rewards behavior.

SENTENCE SENSE HANDOUT

Communication,	teamwork,	and
problem solving	are	effective
ways	to	reinforce
key	session	concepts

15. Brain Teasers

Time Required	10 minutes
Purpose	To energize learners and stimulate the brain while providing a brief break from session content.
Objective(s)	Through a fun and novel activity, the facilitator will be able to:

- Provide a quick mental challenge to learners;

- Energize learners after a period of tedious content;

- Introduce a level of friendly competition to a session; and

- Encourage interpersonal communication.

Group Size	Twenty-five
Process	Use this activity to encourage communication and energize learners at the end of a break or lunch.

Prior to the start of a session, reproduce the Brain Teasers Handout on paper of various colors.

Prior to learners leaving the room on a break or for lunch, tell them that there will be brain-teaser puzzles on their chairs when they return and that the person who finds the correct answers first before the session starts will win a prize (such techniques can encourage learners to return on time).

Explain that the first person finding all the answers should yell, "Done!"

While learners are gone, place handouts on their chairs.

As learners return from break or lunch, tell them they can begin working on the brain teasers.

Once someone has completed all the puzzles, review answers and reward the successful learner with candy or a small prize.

Share correct answers with the rest of the group.

Process Follow-Up	None.

Option(s)	This activity can also be done in small groups to encourage team building and interpersonal communication.
Props/Tools Needed	• Brain Teaser Handouts on various colored paper; and
	• Candy or small prizes.
Possible Topic Application	Unlimited
Why It Is Brain-Based	Adds challenge;
	Stimulates both left and right sides of the brain;
	Adds friendly competition;
	Incorporates novelty and fun into the learning environment;
	Appeals to auditory and visual learners; and
	Uses color that can stimulate the brain.

Brain Teasers Handout

Brain Teasers Answers

1. Adverb
2. One for the Money
3. Up and at 'em
4. Hit and run
5. Excite
6. House of the rising sun
7. Cat's meow
8. Disco dancing
9. Talk of the town
10. Slap in the face
11. High ball
12. Half-hearted

16. Getting Down with the Sound

Time Required 50 minutes

Purpose To energize learners and tie into session content using music.

Objective(s) Through the use of a fun music-based activity, the facilitator will be able to:

- Engage learners in a group activity;
- Reinforce learning content; and
- Foster team collaboration.

Group Size Up to twenty-four

Process Prior to the start of the session, select a well-known song. This can be a current hit from the radio or other well-known verses ("Happy Birthday," "Mary Had a Little Lamb," "Somewhere Over the Rainbow," or "Don't Worry, Be Happy").

Make copies of the words to each of the songs chosen and give a copy to each group leader for use during the activity.

When ready to begin the activity, form equal-sized teams (for example, if you have twenty-four learners, four team of six learners; See Creatively Forming Groups in the Introduction).

Select a leader (spokesperson, facilitator, and timekeeper) and scribe (note-taker) for each group (see Creatively Selecting Volunteers in the Introduction).

Explain that each team is to create a song by modifying the words to a popular song (whatever you have selected).

Considering the fact that there may be learners from different cultures who may not be familiar with the selected song, you might want to have everyone in the room sing it before having them begin the activity, or play a recording of the song so that everyone knows what the goal is.

Once everyone is sure of the task, explain that they will have 30 minutes to come up with a version of the selected song that incorporates as many of the session concepts as possible in the lyrics.

Tell leaders that they should monitor time and that scribes will be responsible for capturing lyrics on a sheet of paper as they are developed and later transfer them to a flip chart so the team can follow along as the song is sung.

To expedite things, you may want to show a flip chart or slide that has the activity guidelines bulleted so that learners can refer to them as they work.

At the 15-minute point and again at the 2-minute-remaining point, sound a noisemaker to attract attention and let learners know the time and answer any questions they have. At this point, determine whether additional time will be needed and adjust accordingly.

At 30 minutes, sound a noisemaker or play music to attract attention and regroup learners.

Have each group leader gather his or her group together and then lead them in their version of the song.

After each rendition, have everyone offer a round of applause.

Option Instead of selecting a song for groups, allow them to choose any song they desire and then have them proceed as outlined in the original activity.

Process Follow-Up *Ask:* "What do you think was the purpose of this activity?"

Possible Answers: Review and reinforce key session concepts;

Involve learners in the learning process;

Give a mental break;

Have a bit of fun; or

Give an opportunity to work as teams.

Ask: "How were music and verse used to reinforce learning during this activity?"

"What key concepts were reviewed through the use of your songs?" (answers will depend on what they chose to include in their songs).

Answer any questions learners have about the activity or session concepts.

Have everyone give one more "encore" round of applause for their great performances.

Props/Tools Needed	• Flip-chart paper;
	• Various colored markers;
	• Masking tape;
	• A copy of the selected song lyrics for each group;
	• Recording of the selected song (if you decide to play it); and
	• CD or other player (as needed).
Possible Topic Application	Any session in which you want to review key concepts or where interpersonal communication, creativity, or teamwork are desired outcomes.
Why It Is Brain-Based	Engages learners mentally and causes memory access as concepts are selected for use in songs;
	Taps both left- and right-brain thinking;
	Appeals to visual and auditory learners;
	Involves several of Gardner's multiple intelligences (bodily/kinesthetic, musical, linguistic, and interpersonal);
	Incorporates color;
	Adds sound and music; and
	Uses novelty and fun.

17. Cross-Laterals

Time Required 5 minutes

Purpose To provide a quick physical and mental break from learning.

Objective(s) Through the use of an active energizer activity, the facilitator will be able to:

- Help learners become more mentally alert;

- Actively involve learners; and

- Provide a diversion from learning.

Group Size Unlimited, based on space available.

Process When ready to conduct the activity, have everyone stand or position themselves so that they have a bit of space to move and bend without hitting objects or other learners.

Explain that cross-lateral activities work because researchers know that each hemisphere of the brain controls the opposite side of the body. Thus, when engaging the left side of the brain and the right side of the body and then the right side of the brain and left side of the body, you are getting a whole-body workout.

Before starting, tell learners to participate only to their own level of comfort or ability and that if something seems too strenuous that they are to modify it as they desire, but to try to participate to some degree.

Have learners face you and tell them to follow your instructions as they do a bit of movement and stretching to re-energize themselves and their brains (because blood flow to the brain increases as they engage the body).

Have learners start by walking in place for 30 seconds while pumping their arms back and forth from front to back.

Have learners continue by raising their left knees and touching their right elbows to their knees (or as close as possible) three times.

Alternate and have them raise their right knees and touch their left elbows to them three times.

Next, have them reach across the front of their bodies with their right hands and pat their left shoulders three times.

Alternate and have them reach across their bodies with their left hands and pat their right shoulders three times.

Raise their left feet behind the right knees and pat the soles of their left feet with their right hands three times.

Raise their right feet behind their left knees and pat the soles of their right feet with their left hands three times.

Have them next stand on tiptoes and reach and stretch as high as they can while shaking their hands in the air, then relax back onto the soles of their feet with their hands back to their sides three times.

Finally, have learners pat the tops of their heads with their left hands while rubbing their stomachs with their right hands at the same time!

Have everyone give a round of applause and have a seat.

Remind learners the importance of taking a break periodically from whatever task they are doing in the workplace or elsewhere so that the body and mind can recharge to increase productivity.

Option(s)
1. Use as often as necessary during sessions, alternating the movements; you may also want to play some sort of upbeat music quietly in the background as you proceed.

2. As an alternative to more active movements that some learners may not be able to do, have everyone stand and, on your command, take ten slow deep breaths while they reach as high as they can, then exhale and drop their hands to their sides and shake them vigorously.

3. Try slow stretches where learners bend at the waist and slowly reach as far as they can toward the floor. This can be done standing or seated.

Note   Because of legal liability and people's personal preferences, be careful about having learners touch others (massaging shoulders and so forth).

Props/Tools Needed	None.
Possible Topic Application	Unlimited.
Why It Is Brain-Based	Engages learners mentally and physically;
	Stimulates blood flow, which aids brain functioning;
	Adds fun and novelty to the environment; and
	Engages Gardner's bodily/kinesthetic intelligence level and, if music is used, the musical intelligence.

18. What's My Issue?

Time Required	45 minutes
Purpose	To engage customer service employees in a fun activity that allows them to get to know one another while allowing them to interact and relax.
Objective(s)	Through a classic fun and non-threatening activity, the facilitator will be able to:

- Encourage interaction;

- Involve learners in addressing workplace issues; and

- Allow learners to practice interpersonal skills.

Group Size	Twenty-four
Process	Prior to the start of the session, write the names of common customer service environment issues that everyone in the group is likely to be familiar with (customer loyalty, dispute resolution, technology, diversity, stress, service recovery, or time management) onto stick-on type nametags. It is okay to have duplicates if necessary.

When ready to start the activity, place one nametag on the back of each learner without letting the person see what is written on it.

Tell them they have 10 minutes to determine what is written on their nametags.

Explain that they are to walk around the room meeting people and that they may ask each person they meet one closed-end question (one that can be answered "yes" or "no").

Tell them that their goal is to determine what their nametags say and that, when they have figured it out, they are to confirm their suspicions with the last person they questioned, then shout out, "I know!" if they are correct.

Reward anyone who is correct with a small prize.

If no one has figured out his or her nametag content within the allotted time, sound a noisemaker or play some upbeat music to attract attention, have them remove their nametags and see what was written on them, and then sit down.

Process Follow-Up	*Ask:* "What was the biggest challenge in this activity? Why was that?"

Possible Answers: Not being able to ask open-ended questions or asking the wrong questions or time constraints.

Ask: "What can you take away from this activity that will be useful in your workplace?"

Possible Answers: It is important to ask the right types of questions to gain information; interpersonal relationship skills are crucial for personal success; it is important to not only listen to what others tell us, but to analyze their responses; we sometimes make assumptions based on partial information, which can lead to incorrect decisions.

Go around the room and have each learner provide one idea for addressing the customer service issue that was on his or her back.

Have everyone give a round of applause for their efforts.

Option(s)
1. Instead of using this activity as an energizer, use it as an opening ice-breaker to introduce concepts that will be covered in a session on customer service skills; or

2. Substitute key session concepts that have been addressed and use this as an interim review or final review by having learners try to guess what key learning concept is on their backs.

Props/Tools Needed
- Nametags with information written on them;

- Noisemaker (bell, whistle, hand clapper, gong, or music); and

- Small prizes or candy for rewards.

Possible Topic Application   You can adapt the activity to virtually any topic by changing the theme.

Why It Is Brain-Based   Actively engages learners mentally and physically;

Causes learners to access memory and reflect on previous knowledge;

Appeals to visual, auditory, and kinesthetic learners;

Applies to several of Gardner's multiple intelligences (linguistic, bodily/kinesthetic, musical, and interpersonal); and

Uses sound/music to add to the environment.

19. Let's Get Together

Time Required	20 minutes
Purpose	To review or discuss key session-related topics.
Objective(s)	Through a random pairing process, the facilitator will be able to:

- Actively engage learners; and

- Create an environment in which learners collaborate on a topic.

Group Size	Up to twenty-four
Process	Prior to the start of the session, obtain a deck of standard playing cards.

Based on the number of learners scheduled for the session, randomly select half as many playing cards (24 learners = 12 cards) and cut them in half horizontally, diagonally, or vertically.

When ready to start the activity, pass out one-half of a card to each learner and tell them not to show them to others.

Explain that they will have 10 to 15 minutes (depending on the topic you assign) to find the person holding the other half of the card that matches theirs and introduce themselves.

They are also to discuss whatever topic you identify for them (for example, one thing they have learned in the session that will be useful to them, a situation in the past where something learned today would have been helpful, or one challenge they see in using something learned today and how they might overcome that challenge).

At the end of the designated time, sound a noisemaker to attract attention and assemble the group.

Process Follow-Up *Ask:* "What did you learn in the activity that might be useful to you in the workplace?"

"What thoughts went through your heads related to today's session content as you talked with your partners?"

Option(s)	1. You can use this activity as an opening icebreaker. Each learner receives half a card as they enter the room and they are to locate the person holding their matching card pieces, introduce themselves, and share one thing about themselves that they think is important (this can be personal or workplace-related information). After time expires, have everyone take a seat. Ask for and reward a volunteer who will start by introducing his or her partner and share what he or she found out. Proceed around the room either left or right until everyone else has introduced a partner; or
	2. Use the activity as either an interim or final review to go over key session concepts by following the guidelines outlined in the original activity above.
Props/Tools Needed	• Playing cards cut in half;
	• Noisemaker (whistle, hand clappers, gong, or bell); and
	• Small prizes or candy.
Possible Topic Application	Any session in which your goal is to get learners involved with each other sharing session-related ideas.
Why It Is Brain-Based	Engages learners mentally and physically;
	Adds sound to the environment;
	Uses an approach of pairing and discussion starting;
	Appeals to auditory learners; and
	Causes learners to access memory and reflect on what they have learned and, depending on the questions asked during processing, how they might apply what they learned.

20. Pass It Along

Time Required	20 to 30 minutes, depending on option chosen
Purpose	To encourage group interaction and problem solving.
Objective(s)	Through the use of a fun activity, the facilitator will be able to:

- Engage learners;

- Provide a means of encouraging inter-group communication; and

- Encourage cooperation and teamwork.

Group Size	Up to twenty-four
Process	Prior to the start of the session, blow up several balloons.

When ready to start the activity, form two equal-sized groups. If there are fewer than ten learners, use one group.

Have each group form a circle in whatever manner they choose. Allow group members to decide whether they stand (side-by-side facing into the center, side-by-side facing away from one another, or front to back facing either right or left), sit in chairs, or sit on the floor.

Ask for a volunteer leader.

Explain that the leader will be given a balloon to start.

When you yell GO, the leader is to start by passing the balloon between both of his or her knees and on to the next person (participants decide which direction to pass).

Note If you have a learner with physical impairments, make appropriate adjustments to the instructions and let all participants know to participate to their level of comfort without drawing attention to any specific learner.

Tell learners that they have 1 minute to accomplish the task of getting the balloon all the way back to the leader and through his or her legs (all group members must pass the balloon as indicated) and that you will sound a noisemaker to signal time is up.

Note   If there are fewer than twelve people in a group, take 5 seconds off the allotted time for each person below that number (for example, ten learners = 50 seconds allotted, eight learners = 40 seconds and so on).

Answer any questions other than providing a solution of how to best accomplish the task.

Yell "GO!" and watch the fun.

At 1 minute, sound a noisemaker to end the activity.

Ask: "With a show of hands, how many groups were successful in accomplishing the task?"

Give a round of applause for any successful groups.

Ask: "Do you think you can do it faster?"

Explain that they may confer among their group members for 2 minutes to discuss how they might do the task differently to accomplish the goal.

At the end of 2 minutes, sound a noisemaker and tell them to get ready to try again.

Yell "GO!" and time the event.

Sound a noisemaker at the end of 1 minute.

Ask: "With a show of hands, how many groups were successful in accomplishing the task?"

Give a round of applause for any successful groups.

Ask: "Do you think you can do it even faster?"

If they indicate that they can go faster, repeat the activity again.

Process Follow-Up   *Ask:* "What was easy about this activity?"

"What was difficult about this activity?"

"How did you overcome any difficulties to achieve your goal?"

"Were you successful the first time? Why or why not?"

"How do you feel about the level of teamwork within the group?"

"What communication took place during the activity that made your group either successful or unsuccessful?"

Reward the group leaders with candy or small prizes.

Have everyone give a round of applause for their efforts.

Option(s)
1. Instead of forming a circle, describe the task (passing the ball through the knees of each group member) and give groups 5 minutes to discuss ways to accomplish the task. Have each group form in whatever manner they have decided; yell "GO!" and allow 1 minute for groups to complete the task. Sound a noisemaker at the end of 1 minute and debrief the activity;

2. Use Koosh®, beach, Nerf®, or other soft balls instead of a balloon, but follow the same guidelines as stated above; or

3. Use the activity as an interim or final review and add more depth to the activity by requiring each learner to shout out one concept or idea that he or she has heard or experienced since being in the session as the ball or balloon is passed to the next person.

Note
An added benefit of balloons is that they sometimes pop, which means teams will fail. This can be related to how pre-planned things sometimes fail in the workplace or life and require a backup plan.

Props/Tools Needed
• Balloons or balls; and

• Small prizes or candy.

Possible Topic Application(s)
Any session in which outcomes such as group interaction, interpersonal communication, and problem solving are desired.

Why It Is Brain-Based
Mentally and physically engages learners;

Requires teamwork, process thinking, problem solving, and decision making;

Ties to several of Gardner's multiple intelligences (bodily/kinesthetic, interpersonal, linguistic, and spatial);

Uses color (balloons or balls); and

Adds eustress (time limits).

21. Team Scavenge

Time Required	30 to 40 minutes, depending on which option is used
Purpose	To provide an activity that can be used to enhance teamwork while accomplishing session-related goals.
Objective(s)	Through the use of a scavenger hunt, the facilitator will be able to:

- Mentally and physically engage learners; and

- Facilitate interpersonal communication and group dynamics.

Group Size	Ten or more (depending on space available)
Process	Prior to the start of the session, make copies of the Scavenger Hunt List or create one of your own.

Begin the activity by forming equal-sized groups of five to ten learners (see Creatively Forming Groups in the Introduction).

Disperse teams around the room/space available so that there is equal distance between them.

Randomly select team leaders (spokesperson, facilitator, and timekeeper) for each group (see Creatively Selecting Volunteers in the Introduction) and have them position themselves in the center of the room separated by an equal amount of space so that items can be placed before them.

Team leaders will be given lists of items that their teams must find. The leaders must remain in place throughout the activity, monitor time, control the list, and verify accuracy of items obtained, but cannot contribute items themselves.

Tell learners that they will be participating in a team scavenger hunt.

Stress that time and creativity are important.

There will be 20 minutes allowed to find all the items on the list given to team leaders.

To find out what is on the list, one person from each team will visit the leader, obtain the name of *one* item (team leaders should not disclose more than one item per visit), go back to get the item from group members, then return to place it in front of the team leader.

Once an item has successfully been placed in front of a leader and the person who obtained it goes back to his or her team area, then a different team member repeats the process, and so on, until all items have been obtained or time ends.

If an item is not available, the team member who obtained the item name will go back to tell the leader that the team cannot find it and obtain the name of a different item, then return to the group and continue the search process.

All team members should participate in identifying and seeking items.

The team with the most items successfully found will be declared the winner and members will receive prizes.

Answer any questions before the activity starts and tell learners that once play begins no further questions will be answered.

Begin play when everyone is ready in their designated team area and leaders have their lists.

Yell "BEGIN" and let the activity start.

Give a 2-minute warning before time is up.

When 20 minutes have elapsed, sound a noisemaker and have everyone stop where they are.

Items that are "in transit" (being carried back to a group leader) can be added to a pile.

Ask: "Did any team find all the items on their list?" (If so, verify they have the correct items and declare any winning team[s]).

Have everyone give a round of applause for their efforts.

Reward the winning team(s) with small prizes (toys or items related to session content are valuable for reinforcing the session content when learners return to their workplace or other environment). You may also want to reward all other participants with small pieces of candy for their efforts, so that there are no losers.

Process Follow-Up   *Ask:* "How many of you got items from sources other than your team members?"

"How many of you went to other teams for items? If you did not, why not?" (No one said they could not do so).

Ask: "What lessons learned from this activity can be transferred back to your workplace?"

Possible Answers: The importance of time management when performing tasks; the role of interpersonal communication when working with others (for instance, questioning and listening); working as a team to successfully complete a project or task; the need to think outside the box and try other things can be helpful when completing a task (such as going to other teams to ask for items or setting up subteams to scour the area for an item to save time rather than one person at a time seeking it); and the importance of obtaining all information about a task prior to beginning it.

Option(s)   You can also use this activity as an interim or final review activity in which the list contains key concepts or ideas learned during the session;

In this case, one team member goes to their leader, obtains a concept, goes back to their group for a definition, and then back to the team leader, who writes down the definition. Play continues with each team member repeating the process until a team has all the correct definitions or time expires. Reward team members of any group that has the most correct concept definitions.

Note   You may want to ask, "Who looked up the concepts in handouts to ensure accurate definitions? If not, why not?" (No one said they could not do so.) Point out that in the workplace it is important to rely on resources for information in order to be successful.

Props/Tools Needed   • Scavenger Hunt List (one for each team leader);

• Small prizes and candy;

• Noisemaker (train whistle, bell, gong, or music); and

• Stopwatch or watch with a second hand.

Possible Topic Application   Sessions in which team interaction, interpersonal communication, problem solving, and time management are desired outcomes.

Why It Is Brain-Based   Involves learners mentally and physically;

Incorporates fun;

Ties to previous learning (possible scavenger hunts as children or in other environments);

Involves several of Gardner's multiple intelligences (interpersonal and bodily/kinesthetic);

Competition is used;

Includes the use of noise and excitement; and

Recognizes and rewards behavior.

Scavenger Hunt List

Instructions: As the leader, you are to monitor time (20 minutes from the time play starts), maintain this list, and disclose only one item at a time as subsequent team members approach to learn the next item on the list.

1. Nickel dated prior to 1995

2. Ink pen with black ink

3. Nail clipper

4. Rubber band

5. Chair

6. Open-toed woman's shoe

7. Belt

8. Foreign coin or currency

9. Paper clip

10. Highlighter marker

11. Band aid

12. Commemorative U.S. quarter from any state south of the Mason-Dixon line

13. Chewing gum (unchewed)

14. Bracelet

15. Cigarette lighter

22. Macarena Coaching

Time Required	45 minutes
Purpose	To provide a lively activity in which learners become mentally and physically involved in a session while reinforcing a number of workplace and life skills.
Objective(s)	Through the use of music and dance, the facilitator will be able to:

- Energize learners;

- Allow learners to practice their coaching and interpersonal skills; and

- Foster teamwork.

Group Size	Up to twenty-four
Process	Prior to the start of the session, acquire a copy of the song "Macarena" by Los del Rio, Los Lobos, or an instrumental version.

Ensure that there is room for all learners working in pairs, and ultimately in lines, to dance the Macarena.

Have learners count off 1, 2, 1, 2, and so on.

Have all the number 2's line up side-by-side somewhere in the room where there is space around them.

Have all the number 1's line up so that each is directly in front of a number 2 at a double arm's length distance.

Explain that each pair should ensure that they have several feet of distance around them in all directions.

Tell learners that the number 1's are going to "teach" their partners the macarena.

Either demonstrate or ask a learner to volunteer to demonstrate the dance without music.

Reward any volunteer with a small prize or session-relevant item.

Following the demonstration, answer any questions learners have.

Next, either demonstrate or have the volunteer do the dance with the music playing (you do not have to play the entire song, just enough to show learners how it is performed).

Explain that if anyone feels he or she cannot perform all the steps or the entire dance, to participate to his or her level of comfort, instruct someone else, and cheer other learners on.

If there is an uneven number of learners, have them form a group of three with one number 1 and two number 2's.

When ready to begin, tell all number 1's that they have 5 minutes to instruct their partners how to do the macarena and have them practice the moves without music.

At the end of 5 minutes, have everyone line up, play the music, and let everyone dance the macarena.

Notes   This activity is best used in group settings where everyone is comfortable with one another or have worked together for a while in order to avoid feelings of embarrassment.

Make sure that you receive permission to use any copyrighted material before using it (see Web Resources/Music Licensing in the Resources section).

Process Follow-Up   *Ask:* "What was your reaction to this activity? Why?"

"What was the most difficult part for each of you? Why?"

"What was the easiest part for each of you? Why?"

"What personal knowledge or attributes did you use to coach your partner on correctly executing the dance?"

Possible Answers: Communication skills; personal experience in coaching others or seeing others coach (sports, training, educational, or environment); patience; listening skills.

Ask: "What lessons can be taken back to the workplace from this activity?"

Possible Answers: If you open your mind to possibilities you can sometimes do things you thought were not possible; learning does not have to be boring; learning from peers can be fun and valuable; communication (speaking clearly, listening, questioning, and feedback) are important skills when teaching someone a task.

Answer any questions that learners have.

Have everyone give themselves a round of applause for their efforts.

Option(s)	If you prefer not to use a dance, have learners teach one another some simple task (putting on a piece of clothing, making a paper airplane that will fly, teaching a limerick or short poem).
Props/Tools Needed	• Music; • CD/cassette player; and • Small rewards.
Possible Topic Application	Any session in which teamwork, interpersonal communication, or task understanding are crucial outcomes.
Why It Is Brain-Based	Ties into Gardner's multiple intelligences (musical, bodily/kinesthetic, and interpersonal); Actively engages learners; Appeals to visual, auditory, and kinesthetic learners; Incorporates music and sound, which can enhance the learning environment; and Recognizes and rewards behavior.

SECTION 3

Interim Reviews

"Creative minds have always been known to survive any kind of bad training."

—Anna Freud

Overview

Memory is aided by repetition. The more times you see, hear, taste, touch, or smell something, the more likely you are to obtain information and knowledge about it, retain it, and recall it later for use. This is why frequent review activities are crucial.

Too often, trainers and educators wait until the end of a learning event to review content. At that point it is too late to go back and re-teach any important concepts missed or misunderstood; thus, learners walk away without meeting learning objectives and having wasted their time. This is why creative interim and final reviews can be fun and beneficial steps in the memory process. They provide quick ways to help learners better grasp and retain session content for later recall and application. They also help facilitators identify any content that needs further attention and emphasis.

Games and Activities in This Section

23. Let Me Tell You a Story

Time Required	10 minutes
Purpose	To provide an opportunity to create a story based on key session concepts and stimulate communication during a learning event.
Objective(s)	Through the use of spontaneous storytelling, the facilitator will be able to:

- Allow learners to review session content by creating a story based on what they have learned during the session;

- Encourage interpersonal communication; and

- Prompt creativity.

Group Size	Twenty-five
Process	Have learners form small equal-sized circles.

Give one person a ball made of soft material (for example, Koosh®, Noodle®, sponge, Nerf®, or similar type).

Inform learners that, when told to begin, the person holding the ball will begin a story related to the session topic, using a phrase or word learned in the session.

The first person will pass the ball to the person on his or her left, who will add a phrase or word related to the program, then pass the ball along to the person on the left. For example, if the session were focused on team building, the first person might start, "The great thing about team building," the second person might add, "is that it increases communication," the third person might contribute, "so that we can deliver effective customer service," and so on.

Continue the process until learner stories seem to bog down or until 5 minutes have passed.

Sound a noisemaker to regain attention and signal the end of the event.

Process Follow-Up   *Ask:* "How many of you had difficulty adding to the story? Why was that?"

"What key session concepts were tied into this activity?"

"What did you do during this activity that might be useful in the work-place?" (for example, tying into the ideas of others or relating current events to past learning or knowledge).

Have everyone give a round of applause for their efforts.

Reward all learners with candy or small prizes for their creativity.

Option(s)   1. Change the purpose of the activity to just energize and have learners create a story with no defined topic or focus by having each person say only one word before passing the ball to the next person, who adds another word, and so on. This encourages creativity, evokes laughter, and stimulates the brain as they struggle to keep the story going. This option is perfect for sessions relating to communication, team building, or other relationship topics.

2. Instead of having learners stand to form a circle, have them do the activity on paper by passing from one person to the next under strict time constraints (for example, no one can keep the paper more than 15 seconds). This approach is not as physical but evokes excitement and laughter as people scurry to complete the task and keep the story going.

Props/Tools Needed   • Koosh® or other soft type of ball;

• Noisemaker; and

• Small prizes or candy.

Possible Topic Application   Unlimited.

Why It Is Brain-Based   Encourages memory and recall;

Actively engages learners;

Appeals to auditory learners; and

Incorporates fun into a review activity.

24. Pass the Pickle

Time Required	10 minutes
Purpose	To provide a humorous way to review key session concepts.
Objective(s)	Through the use of a musical prop, the facilitator will be able to:

- Engage learners physically and mentally; and

- Create a fun environment in which learners can review key concepts of the session.

Group Size	Up to seventy-five
Process	Have participants form equal-sized circles facing one another (see Creatively Forming Groups in the Introduction).

Tell them that they are going to be reviewing key concepts, ideas, and issues raised during the session.

Hand one person in each group a Musical Pickle.

Explain that when the music starts (by pushing the button on the bottom) the person with the pickle is to shout out one key idea or concept that he or she has gained from any source during the session, related to the program topic.

The person with the pickle will then quickly pass it to the person on his or her left, who will repeat the process.

This will continue until the music stops.

The person holding the pickle when the music stops shouts out an idea, hands the pickle to the person on his or her left, and then sits down.

Tell learners that they cannot repeat anything someone has already said.

Continue the process until only one person remains.

Reward the last person with a small prize (for example, a plastic toy trophy).

Process Follow-Up	Review any additional key concepts not covered by learners in the review.

Have everyone give a round of applause for their efforts.

Ask: "How can the concepts learned in this session be applied in the workplace?"

Option(s):

1. When using the activity in a group of more than twelve learners, form two groups and, after both groups have only one member remaining, form a single circle and continue until one person remains standing. Reward the final person with a small prize and have everyone give themselves a round of applause for their great ideas; or

2. If you only have one group, designate one learner as the scribe who captures each idea shouted on a flip-chart page so learners can see what has been stated and not repeat concepts. Since this activity moves rather quickly, if you do this, you might have two flip charts so that you can assist in capturing terms or concept on paper. Every other term or concept shouted is written on alternate pages (you capture the first idea, the scribe captures the second, you write the third, and so on).

Props/Tools Needed

- Musical Pass the Pickle for each group (see Resources);

- Flip chart(s);

- Assorted colored markers; and

- Candy or small prizes.

Possible Topic Application

Any session in which interpersonal communication or teamwork are desired outcomes or for which you desire to review key session concepts.

Why It Is Brain-Based

Fun, humor and novelty used;

Adds element of competition;

Reinforces key concepts in memory;

Addresses auditory, visual and kinesthetic learner needs;

Recognizes and rewards behavior;

Introduces music and color (pickle) into the environment.

25. Balloon Review

Time Required   10 minutes

Purpose   To provide an upbeat and fun means of reviewing key session concepts.

Objective(s)   Using colorful balloons as props, the facilitator will be able to:

- Introduce a non-threatening and fun way to review session content;

- Reinforce key learning concepts and objectives; and

- Identify any key concepts not learned so that they can be re-taught or reinforced before moving on to more content.

Group Size   Twenty-five

Process   Prior to the start of the session, type or write key concepts covered in the session thus far onto small strips of paper (one concept per strip).

Place the strips of paper inside balloons and blow them up; then tape them to the walls around your room.

When ready to conduct the review activity, have each participant take a balloon from the wall and return to his or her seat, but remain standing.

Tell them that inside their balloons are strips of paper with key concepts covered thus far in the session.

When you say "Go," have them pop their balloons and recover their review strips.

Ask for a volunteer to read his or her strip (reward this first person and say, "With initiative, comes reward in training"). Then have the person define the term based on what was covered in class.

Tell others they can add to what the person says.

In turn, each person will read his or her strip and define the term (same procedure as before).

Process Follow-Up   *Ask:* "What do you think is the most important concept learned thus far? Why do you think so?"

"What other key concepts or ideas have you learned thus far from the session that you think will be valuable in the workplace?"

Have everyone give a round of applause for their efforts and great answers.

Option(s)

1. Use as an opening icebreaker. Have each person introduce him- or herself and read his or her strip. Ask the group what they think the concept means. This allows a quick assessment of what areas you need to focus on during the session;

2. If you are using this activity as an interim review and there are not enough key concepts covered to have one in each balloon, leave some balloons empty and tell learners that not everyone will find a strip in his or her balloon. This approach still allows everyone to move to retrieve a and pop a balloon;

3. Use as an opening activity in which you place the session objectives in balloons and ask for volunteers to retrieve and read them after they introduce themselves. After each one is read, give a brief description of how you will accomplish each objective. Once all objectives have been read, ask the remaining learners to introduce themselves in turn;

4. If there are more balloons and concepts than learners in the session, once all participants have selected balloons and defined terms, pop any remaining balloons and ask everyone for the definition of the terms; or

5. If you do not have enough covered concepts at the scheduled time of the review activity (for example, you are doing an interim review in the morning), just use enough balloons for what you have and ask for that many volunteers to retrieve the balloons and read the strips. Reward these volunteers.

Props/Tools Needed

- Various colored balloons;

- Small paper strips with key concepts;

- Masking tape; and

- Candy or small prizes.

Possible Topic Application	Unlimited.
Why It Is Brain-Based	Engages learners physically and mentally;
	Adds fun and novelty to the review process;
	Incorporates color (balloons) into the environment;
	Adds noise and an air of excitement as the balloons are popped to find what is inside (ties to early childhood experiences of opening a package to discover what was inside);
	Taps into memory and recall; and
	Appeals to visual, auditory, and kinesthetic learners.

26. Roll of the Dice

Time Required   20 minutes

Purpose   To provide an upbeat and fun means of reviewing key session concepts.

Objective(s)   Through the use of a pair of dice, the facilitator will be able to:

- Creatively engage learners in a review of key session learning concepts; and

- Provide an energizing means of involving learners.

Group Size   Unlimited.

Process   Prior to the session, create a numbered list of two to twelve key session concepts on a sheet of colored paper. Also create a second list on a different color paper, with definitions that correlate to the numbered concepts on the first list. Fold both lists separately and place a copy inside an envelope (one envelope with both lists per group).

Form groups of eight to ten learners (see Creatively Forming Groups in the Introduction).

Select a group leader for each group (see Creatively Selecting Volunteers in the Introduction). Explain that their role is to monitor time and assist the group through the process.

Give each group leader a pair of dice and an envelope.

Explain that learners have 10 minutes to review key concepts using the dice.

When ready to begin, have the group leaders start by rolling the dice.

Explain that, after rolling, the leader is to take the list with the definitions from the envelope, read the definition that has the same number as the dice rolled, and have someone try to identify the concept. The leader can verify correctness by looking at the second list.

If the learner answering was correct, the leader will say so; if not, other group members will be encouraged to guess the answer.

The process continues, with other members of the group rolling the dice and the leader reading definitions and so on until all concepts have been covered.

If a dice number is rolled for a concept that has already been selected, the person will continue to roll until a number not covered thus far comes up.

Once all terms have been covered, the group leader will shout "Finished!" and members of that group can be rewarded with candy or small gifts.

Reward all leaders as well with candy or small prizes.

Process Follow-Up   Cover any additional key terms that were not covered by the activity.

Ask: "What questions do you have about anything we have covered thus far in the session?"

"How can the concepts learned in this session be applied in the workplace?"

Have everyone give a round of applause for their efforts.

Option(s)   1. Do the activity as one large group. Ask for two volunteers to roll one die each (use a die large enough to be seen from a distance 4 inches, 8 inches, or 16 inches square). Read definitions based on dice numbers rolled; ask the group for volunteers to define the concepts; and reward volunteers who provide correct answers with candy or small prizes; or

2. If you have twenty-five or fewer learners, instead of using this as a small group activity, put the concepts and clues on slides or flip-chart paper, read one at a time, and have anyone with the answer raise a hand to be recognized. Reward volunteers with candy or prizes.

Props/Tools Needed   • Dice (size depends on option selected);

• Two different colors of copy paper with definitions and concepts typed on them;

• Envelopes for each group (depending on which option is selected);

• Slides or flip-chart paper (option 2); and

• Assorted colored markers (option 2).

Possible Topic Application	Any session in which teamwork, interpersonal communication, and concept review are desired outcomes.
Why It Is Brain-Based	Incorporates novelty and fun;
	Uses color (paper and dice) to stimulate the brain;
	Cause learners to reflect and access memory;
	Engages learners physically and mentally;
	Appeals to visual, auditory, and kinesthetic learners;
	Recognizes and rewards behavior; and
	Ties to previous life experiences (use of dice and games).

27. I've Got Your Number

Time Required	15 minutes
Purpose	To allow learners an opportunity to review key program concepts during a session.
Objective(s)	Through the use of random selection, the facilitator will be able to:

- Engage learners mentally; and
- Reinforce key elements of the session.

Group Size	Twenty-five
Process	Prior to the learning event, create a list of definitions for key concepts covered during the session, along with correct responses.

When ready to start the review activity, pass out one carnival-type coupon ticket (use the double-roll type for which you keep one ticket and give learners one with the exact same number).

Tell learners that they are now going to review key concepts through use of the tickets.

Select one ticket randomly and read the number. The learner holding the matching numbered ticket will have an opportunity to identify a key concept based on the definition that you will read.

If the person chosen cannot identify the concept, any other learner can volunteer to answer.

Repeat the process until all key concepts have been read, or all learners have participated. Any remaining concepts that were not covered can be read and anyone can respond.

Throughout the review, reward correct responses with candy or small prizes related to the concept theme (for example, customer service classes might use items with smile faces on them).

Process Follow-Up   *Ask:* "What other key concepts or ideas have you learned thus far in the session?"

"How can the concepts learned in this session be applied in the workplace?"

"What questions do you have about anything covered thus far?"

Have everyone give a round of applause for their answers and participation.

Option(s)   1. Pass out coupons throughout the session for learners being on time, responding correctly, volunteering, or whatever other behavior you desire to reward. When ready to conduct the review, randomly select tickets and process as in original activity;

2. Prior to the start of a session with fewer than twenty-four learners, attach one coupon of a pair to a small paper bag that contains a concept definition and a small toy or other prize (have enough bags for all learners to receive one). As learners arrive, give each a ticket that matches one of the pair attached to the bags.

   When ready to review session content, have learners in turn read their numbers and give them the corresponding bags. The learner receiving a bag will open it, read the definition, and attempt to identify the correct concept. If the person succeeds, he or she keeps the prize. Otherwise, it goes back into a pile in the center of the table or room.

   Continue until all bags have been opened and concepts defined. Once every learner has defined a term, ask a general question of everyone in the room that relates to how they might apply a crucial session concept to their workplace. The learner who volunteers first and knows the correct answer may keep any prizes collected in the center of the table or room.

   Have everyone give a round of applause for their efforts; or

3. Instead of coupons, use colored strips of paper that you have created with duplicate numbers on and follow the process outlined for the original activity above.

Props/Tools Needed	• Carnival double-roll coupons or colored strips of paper with numbers on them;
	• Small prizes or candy; and
	• Paper bags (option 2).

Possible Topic Applications Unlimited.

Why It Is Brain-Based Involves random selection/chance;

Adds fun and novelty to the environment;

Engages learners mentally;

Recognizes and rewards behavior; and

Causes reflection and recall from memory.

28. Take a Pick

Time Required	10 minutes
Purpose	To allow learners an opportunity to review key program concepts during a session.
Objective(s)	Through an interactive approach, the facilitator will be able to:

- Provide a vehicle for learners to recall and review key session concepts; and

- Engage learners.

Group Size	Twenty-five
Process	Prior to the start of the session, create a deck of 3-by-5 cards on which each has one key concept or idea from the session.

When ready to begin the review activity, allow each learner to select one card from the deck. Explain that each card contains a concept or idea covered during the session.

They will in turn read their concepts, describe what it means, and tell how they think it applies to their workplace.

Tell the group that anyone may offer additional information about a concept if something is left out.

Ask for a volunteer, reward him or her, and begin the review process.

Continue until all learners have participated.

Process Follow-Up	After all learners have identified and defined their concepts, offer any other key concepts that are important for learners to remember;

Ask: "How can the concepts learned in this session be applied in the workplace?"

At the end of the review, have everyone give a round of applause for their efforts.

Option(s)

1. Use the activity as an end of session review and, after all learners have read their concepts and defined them, form small, equal-sized groups to have them discuss how they will use their concepts following the session. Allow 15 minutes for discussion, then ask for random volunteers to share how their concepts will be applied. Reward volunteers with small prizes or candy; or

2. Instead of passing the cards out to individuals, form equal-sized groups, give them enough cards for each group member, have them discuss their concepts and then discuss how the concepts might be applied following training. Allow 15 to 20 minutes for discussion. Then sound a noise-maker to regain attention. Ask for random volunteers to share one concept discussed by his or her group and how it might be applied following training; reward the volunteer with a small prize or candy. Have everyone give a round of applause for their efforts.

Props/Tools Needed

- 3-by-5 cards with concepts written on them;

- Noisemaker (music, whistle, bell, gong, or whatever you prefer); and

- Small prizes or candy.

Possible Topic Applications

Unlimited.

Why It Is Brain-Based

Engages learners mentally;

Encourages recall and reflection from memory;

Appeals to auditory learners;

Uses music or sound;

Recognizes and rewards behavior; and

Focuses attention on transfer of knowledge.

29. Let's "Eggs"amine This

Time Required	10 minutes
Purpose	Provide a lighthearted approach to reviewing key session content.
Objective(s)	Through the creative use of plastic eggs, the facilitator will be able to:

- Conduct a novel and fun interim review session;

- Engage learners in the review process; and

- Cause learners to reflect on key session concepts and how they might be applied following training.

Group Size	Twenty-five
Process	Prior to the start of the session, create small strips of paper that have key session concepts typed onto them.

Place the paper strips into two-piece, multi-colored, plastic eggs and put them into a wicker basket, bowl, or bag for distribution later.

If there are not enough concepts covered in the session to fill an egg for each learner, use strips with the question: "How can the last concept identified be used in the workplace?"

When ready to begin the review, pass around the eggs and have each learner take one.

Explain that inside their eggs they will find pieces of paper with key concepts written on them.

Once the activity begins, they are to open their eggs and read what is on their papers, then define the term or concept for the rest of the group.

Ask for a volunteer to open and read his or her egg, then continue around the room in order until all eggs have been opened and the concepts read.

Reward the volunteer with candy or a small prize.

Process Follow-Up   After all learners have opened their eggs and read their concepts, *ask:* "What other key concepts or ideas have you obtained from the session that were not identified during the review?"

"How can the concepts learned in this session be applied in the workplace?"

"What questions do you have thus far about anything we have covered or anything related?"

Have everyone give a round of applause for their efforts during the review.

Option(s)   1. Use as an end of session review of key concepts instead of an interim review.

2. Instead of using as a review activity, place key concepts in the eggs and pass them out during your introduction segment of the session. Have learners take an egg and in turn do a personal introduction, share what is written on the paper inside the egg, then attempt to explain the concept. If they answer correctly, reward them with candy or a small prize. If they cannot answer correctly, ask for anyone else in the group to attempt to do so. If no one can answer, give a brief description of the concept and let them know they will learn more about it later in the session. Have everyone give a round of applause for their efforts; or

3. Instead of using the activity as a review, use it as either an opening ice-breaker or during a program as a conversation starter. Prior to the start of a session, put questions inside the eggs related to the session topic. For example, as an icebreaker in an orientation session use questions like: "What has been your biggest career challenge to date and why?" "Why did you decide to join this organization?" "What product or service offered by this organization do you think is the most unique and why?"

When ready to begin the activity, have learners choose eggs and, in turn, open them, introduce themselves, and then read and answer their questions.

Props/Tools Needed   • Multi-colored two-piece plastic eggs (can be found in party, discount, or department stores);

• Basket, bowl, or bag for eggs;

• Paper strips with either questions or concepts on them; and

• Candy or small prizes for volunteers.

Possible Topic Application	Any session in which interpersonal communication and review of session concepts are desired outcomes.
Why It Is Brain-Based	Adds fun and novelty;
	Causes learners to reflect and recall information from memory;
	Appeals to visual, auditory, and kinesthetic learners;
	Uses color; and
	Incorporates rewards.

30. My Present to You

Time Required	30 minutes
Purpose	To conduct a lighthearted interim review of key concepts.
Objective(s)	Through the use of an upbeat review activity, the facilitator will:

- Provide learners with an opportunity to reflect on key session concepts; and

- Encourage active learner participation in reviewing important session ideas or learning points.

Group Size	Twenty-five
Process	Prior to the start of a session, prepare a sheet of paper (use various colors of paper) with one key idea or concept from the session for each learner. The concepts should be listed at the top of the page, along with a brief description or definition. In the middle of the page, put the statement: "How can you use this concept/idea in the real world?"

Fold each sheet of paper and either wrap it as you would a present in brightly colored wrapping paper or place it in a small brown or white bag (the type used in some bulk candy stores).

When ready to conduct the review, state that you have a "gift" for each person and ask for a volunteer to pass out the "gifts" to all learners.

Reward the volunteer with candy or a small prize.

Tell learners not to open their presents until everyone has one.

Once everyone has a "gift," have them open and read them, then write the answers to the questions on their papers.

Allow 5 minutes to do this.

At 3 minutes, give a 2-minute warning and sound a noisemaker to regain attention when time is up.

Have each learner in turn read his or her concept and response to the question.

Process Follow-Up	Following the review, stress the importance of putting their new knowledge or skills to work right away.

Ask: "Which of these concepts do you think you will be able to immediately use? In what way?"

"What questions do you have about anything covered today?"

Review any key concepts not identified by learners and ask them to define the terms.

Have everyone give a round of applause for their efforts and input.

Note   Following the Process Follow-Up, you may want to give a real gift in the form of a small topic-related toy or prize to each learner for participation in the session.

Option(s)   Instead of using this activity for an interim session review, create an activity that ends a session on a high note. Prior to the session, create a series of "tips" related to session content that you can wrap and give as presents. For example, in a customer service session, you might create twenty-five tips for more effectively serving customers.

After you have completed your session review of key concepts, ask for a volunteer to pass out the presents. Reward the volunteer with candy or a small prize.

Once everyone has a present, have them open and read them in turn to the group. After all presents have been opened and read, have everyone give a round of applause for their contribution.

Pass out single sheets that include all of the tips combined so that everyone will have a future reference.

Props/Tools Needed
- Colored sheets of paper;
- Candy or small prizes;
- Noisemaker (whistle, bells, hand clapper, gong, music, or party favor); and
- Tip sheet (if option 2 is chosen).

Possible Topic Application   Any session in which you desire to review key concepts covered.

Why It Is Brain-Based   Causes reflection and recall of information from memory;

Appeals to visual and auditory learners;

Encourages volunteerism and involvement;

Reinforces key concepts through repetition; and

Uses color (paper).

31. Pop-Up Review

Time Required	15 minutes
Purpose	To provide a quick, energizing interim review of session content.
Objective(s)	Through the use of a fast-moving, creative process, the facilitator will be able to:

- Cause learners to reflect on key concepts covered during the session; and

- Identify key concepts that need further review.

Group Size	Up to twenty-four
Process	Explain to learners that they are going to participate in a quick review of key concepts.

Tell them that you will shout out a key concept or idea covered in the session and the people knowing what it means should jump to their feet (or if they are not able to do so, raise their hands or otherwise signal quickly).

Let them know that anyone giving an answer correctly will receive a prize (candy or small prizes may be used).

Answer any questions learners have about the process and then proceed.

After all terms have been called and defined, have everyone give a round of applause for their efforts.

Process Review	Revisit any key session concepts not covered in the review and ask learners to define the terms;

Ask: "Which of the concepts covered in the session do you think you will be able to immediately use? Why is that?"

"Which concepts might not be readily useful? Why not?"

"What questions do you have about anything covered in the session?"

Option(s)	1. Instead of you calling out terms, start with a volunteer who stands and calls out the first idea or concept he or she remembers from the session. Each learner in turn stands, calls out a concept, then sits back down; any other learner can then stand and define the concept identified. The process continues until all key concepts have been covered. Tell learners at the beginning that they cannot use a concept or idea already called out by someone else. Pass out candy or small rewards to anyone identifying or defining a concept; or
	2. Instead of using this activity as an interim review, use at the end of the session as a final review and follow the process in the original activity.
Props/Tools Needed	Candy or small prizes.
Possible Topic Application	Unlimited.
Why It Is Brain-Based	Adds fun;
	Requires memory access and recall of concepts or previously stored information;
	Mentally and physically engages learners; and
	Recognizes and rewards behavior.

32. Name It

Time Required   30 to 45 minutes (depending on group size)

Purpose   To provide a fast-moving, energizing interim review that focuses on session content.

Objective(s)   Through use of a game loosely modeled after the classic game Password®, the facilitator will be able to:

- Provide an opportunity for learners to revisit key concepts from the session; and

- Create a friendly but competitive atmosphere.

Group Size   From ten to twenty-four

Process   Prior to the start of the session, prepare two stacks of at least twenty-five 3-by-5 index cards with the names of key session terms on them (for example, in an Introduction to Computers session, the terms might include keyboard, monitor, boot, or log on).

Arrange chairs in two large, equal-sized circles and ensure that there is a chair for each learner.

Note   If you have twelve or fewer learners, only use one circle.

When ready to start the activity, form two equal-sized groups of learners (based on the total number of learners).

Have each group proceed to a circle of chairs.

Once everyone is seated, designate a Team 1 and Team 2 in each group by having everyone count off to the right 1, 2, 1, 2, and so on.

Designate one scribe (note-taker) from each team, have them sit next to one another, and provide the Team 1 scribe with a pencil and pad of paper for scoring.

Have the scribe with the pad write "Team 1" and "Team 2" at the top right and left portion of the paper and draw a line vertically down the center to separate the two teams' scoring areas.

Hand one pile of index cards face down to a Team 1 member on the opposite side of the circle from where the scribes are seated.

Tell learners that they will have 2 minutes to play.

Explain that, when you say "Go," the person holding the cards will turn over the top card without showing it to anyone else.

That person will provide clues as to the card's content, but cannot actually say what the word or concept is.

Tell them that they will have 1 minute to provide clues and that only their teammates may guess what is on each card.

If a teammate guesses correctly, the scribe will record 1 point for that team and play stops for that round.

Share with learners that at the end of 1 minute you will sound a noisemaker (demonstrate the sound, such as a bell, buzzer, whistle, etc.) to alert them that time is up if a team is still playing.

Say that, when they hear the sound, all clues and guessing stop; otherwise the opposing team will be awarded 1 point.

The last card used is placed face up at the bottom of the deck if not guessed. If it was guessed, the card is discarded to the side.

After the first round of clues and guesses, the card deck is then passed to the next person to the right and the play continues in like fashion until all cards are guessed or until time has elapsed.

If a team gets to the cards that are face up, they will turn the deck over and continue play.

When the card deck moves to the scribe keeping score, he or she will pass the score pad to the second scribe and scorekeeping responsibilities will temporarily pass to that person until his or her turn to provide clues, at which point it passes back to the Team 1 scribe.

After game time expires, if there are still cards remaining to be guessed, take them and do a quick instructor-led review of those concepts with all learners.

Process Follow-Up	*Ask:* "Which of the concepts that you just reviewed do you feel are the most useful to you? Why is that?"

Which will be the least useful to you? Why?"

Answer any question learners have about content reviewed.

Reward all scribes with candy or small prizes.

Have everyone give a round of applause for their efforts.

Option Instead of an interim review, use this activity as an end-of-session review, using key concepts and following the guidelines above.

Props/Tools Needed
- 3-by-5 index cards;
- Candy or small prizes;
- Pencil and pad of paper; and
- Noisemaker (train whistle, cow bell, or gong)

Possible Topic Application Any activity in which interpersonal communication and a review of key session concepts are desired outcomes.

Why It Is Brain-Based Adds fun and novelty;

Adds noise, which stimulates the brain;

Increase adrenaline and provides friendly competition;

Adds eustress;

Appeals to visual, auditory, and kinesthetic learners;

Requires learners to recall information; and

Recognizes and rewards behavior.

33. Please Give Me a Hand

Time Required	15 minutes
Purpose	To provide learners an opportunity to reflect on key session concepts they have experienced and add a bit of novelty to the session.
Objective(s)	Through the use of a novel interim review activity just before a session break, the facilitator will be able to:

- Allow learners to review session content in a novel manner; and

- Gather feedback on what concepts learners think are important and about the session facilitation.

Group Size	Any size.
Process	Prior to the session starting, create a flip-chart page that looks like the "Please Give Me a Hand" sheet at the end of this activity.
Note	If you do not have artistic talent and do not have access to someone who does, try making a transparency of the sheet, put it on an overhead projector that you project onto a flip-chart page and trace the hand.

Before learners arrive, take the flip-chart page outside or to a well-ventilated area and spray the front of it with repositionable artist's adhesive (sold at arts and craft stores). Then tape the sheet to the back of the classroom exit door or on a wall next to it.

Reproduce the "light bulb" handout onto various colors of bright-colored copy paper and then cut out the bulb images.

When ready to start the review activity, give each learner one light bulb handout.

Explain that during the session they have experienced a number of key concepts and that they are to select the one they believe to be most important or useful to them, then write the concept briefly on the front of the light bulb.

Once everyone has finished, have them turn their bulbs over and write one thing they would do differently if they were facilitating the session. If they cannot think of anything, have learners write "Nothing" on their bulbs.

Give learners 5 minutes to share the key concepts they selected and what they wrote with the persons on either side of them and tell why they selected the terms or concepts.

Tell them that they are going on a break/to lunch now and that on the way out the door, they should place their light bulbs on the Please Give Me a Hand flip-chart page.

While learners are out of the room, gather all the bulbs and read the key concepts to see which they selected.

If it appears that there are key concepts that they should recognize as important, but did not, re-emphasize these concepts when learners return to make sure they heard and understood the concepts.

While learners are out of the room, also look at the things that they indicated they would change. If appropriate, make those changes during the remainder of the session, rather than waiting until the next session. In the latter case, current learners receive no benefits from the changes.

Process Follow-Up   After everyone returns, go around the room and ask for a volunteer to tell which key concept he or she chose for the light bulb and why he or she thinks it is important or useful.

Reward volunteers with candy or small prizes.

Ask: "What did the light bulb review successfully force you to do?"

"What are some of the key session concepts you considered putting on your light bulb, and why did you choose the one you did?"

"How do the key concepts identified in this activity relate to your workplace?"

Have everyone give a round of applause for their efforts.

Option   Instead of using as an interim review of key session concepts, use this activity to gather any information desired during a session (for example, alternative suggestions for session content, possible solutions to a problem presented, questions about the session or content, or answers to a question posed).

Props/Tools Needed	• Cutouts of the light bulb handout on various colors of copy paper;
	• Artist's adhesive;
	• Pre-drawn flip chart of a hand;
	• Masking tape; and
	• Small prizes or candy.
Possible Topic Application	Any session in which you want to gain session feedback and to review key concepts covered.
Why It Is Brain-Based	Engages memory and encourages recall;
	Mentally and physically engages learners;
	Appeals to auditory, visual, and kinesthetic learners;
	Uses color to enhance the learning environment; and
	Incorporates novelty and fun in review.

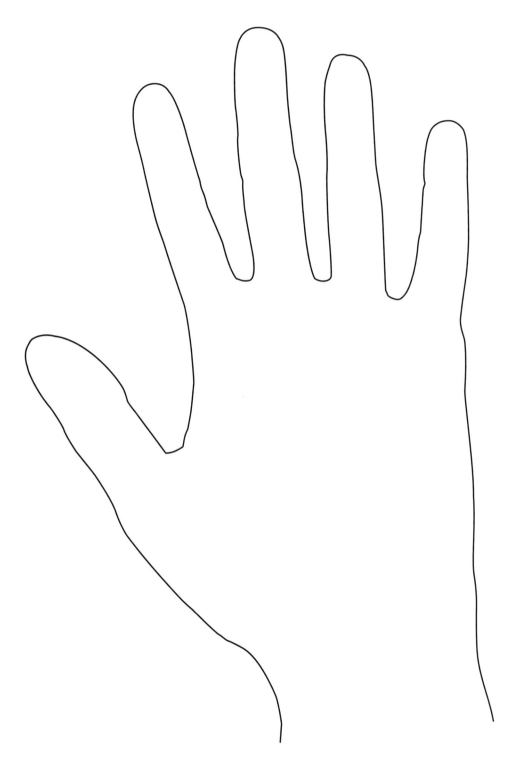

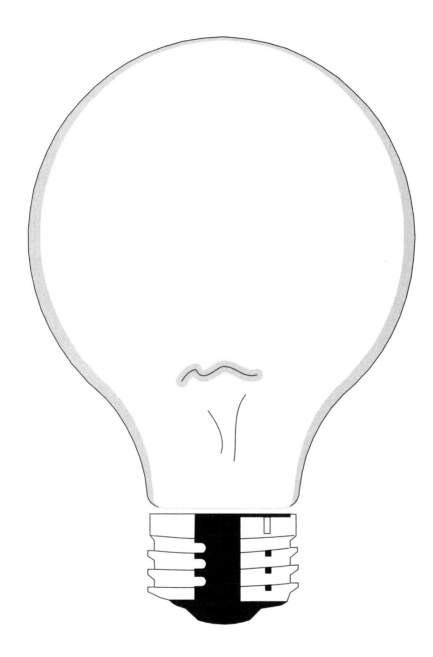

S E C T I O N   4

Transfer of Learning

"For the things we have to learn before we can do them, we learn by doing them."

—Aristotle

Overview

One of the biggest challenges facing anyone who trains or educates others is: "How do I make sure that what they learn is used or makes a difference?" Trainers and educators continually look for ways to make sure that the knowledge and skills they are giving learners will really be useful in the "real world."

Many experienced trainers, educators, and brain researchers have found out that, through such elements as novelty, fun, challenge, competition, and reflection, people are better able to attain, retain, and recall information for later use. Because games and activities can be used to stimulate interest, reinforce key concepts, and help learners grasp information in a fun manner, it makes sense to incorporate them into your learning initiatives.

In this section, you will find games and activities that help with the all-important transfer of learning issue that so many trainers, educators, and meeting facilitators struggle with. It provides useful ways to help learners attain an "ah ha" moment in which they see how the content learned during a particular session will be applicable to their own workplace situations.

Games and Activities in This Section

34. It's Very Simple

Time Required Approximately 15 minutes

Purpose To provide a fun and creative activity that reinforces the importance of effective interpersonal communication skills.

Objective(s) Through a demonstration, the facilitator will be able to help learners:

- Recognize the importance of correctly using effective verbal communication to share information with someone else;

- Identify ways that we sometimes make assumptions about the level of knowledge someone has about a topic when we communicate with him or her; and

- Become aware of the need to plan communication before delivering messages.

Group Size Maximum of fifty

Process Ask for two volunteers to participate in a demonstration.

Give each volunteer a copy of his or her "role" instructions (see handouts at the end of this activity) and allow 3 minutes for the volunteers to read their roles and mentally prepare.

Give all participants copies of each handout so that they will know the scenario.

Place a zippered jacket on a table at the front of the room and position both role players as described in the handouts.

When you tell them to begin, each person will follow the instructions provided until you say "stop" (3 minutes).

Process Follow-Up At the end of the time period, start with the "scientist" by asking the following questions:

- "What did you do that was effective in instructing your partner? Why did it work?"

- "What do you think you did that was not effective? Why didn't it work?"

- "What could you have done differently to make the learning experience more effective for your partner?"

Ask the "tribesperson" the following questions:

- "What did the 'scientist' do effectively in instructing you?"

- "What did he or she do that you think was ineffective?"

- "How could he or she have been more effective?"

Ask other participants in the program:

- "What did you see the scientist do effectively or ineffectively?"

- "How could the instruction have been improved?"

Ask everyone:

- "How will all this apply to situations in which you are communicating with others?"

Option   Have each learner bring a zippered jacket to the class. Have learners form pairs with one assuming each role. When told to begin, have each scientist instruct his or her partner on how to put on a jacket;

After the 5 minutes have elapsed, have everyone switch roles and the former tribespeople will instruct their partners on how to put on a jacket.

Process the activity by asking the questions listed in the original activity above.

Props/Tools Needed   • Zippered jacket (extra large, unless you know the size of your demonstrator in advance); and

• Tribesperson and Scientist handouts (enough for demonstrators and one of each participant so that they know the scenario before the demonstration begins).

Possible Topic Applications

Interpersonal communication	Customer service
Management/supervision	Coaching/mentoring/counseling

Why It Is Brain-Based   Engages visual, auditory, and kinesthetic learners; and

Stimulates learners to assess and analyze the situation and think of ways it applies to them.

It's Very Simple: Scientist's Role

You are a member of a scientific team that has just returned from a formerly unknown and uncharted island in the Pacific with a blind member of a primitive tribe.

Start by standing a few feet behind your role-play partner so that you can see what he or she is doing.

This tribesperson has never seen or worn clothing prior to meeting your team.

Before presenting him or her to colleagues, you need to instruct him or her on proper dress. Up to this point, you have taught the tribesperson how to put on all clothing except for a jacket, which is lying nearby.

Your task is to verbally explain the proper manner to put the jacket on and to zip it up.

You may not touch the jacket or tribesperson or demonstrate in any way (remember that he/she is blind and cannot see you); only verbal instruction is to be used.

He/she will do EXACTLY what you tell him/her to do.

It's Very Simple: Tribesperson's Role

Assume that you are a *blind* member of a primitive Pacific Ocean tribe who has been brought back to the United States by a team of scientists.

Start by standing facing the jacket and with your back to your role-play partner to simulate your blindness and to avoid seeing any nonverbal cues.

You have never seen or worn clothing prior to your contact with the team, but must dress prior to meeting other members of a university staff.

Previously, you have been taught to put on all of your clothing except a zippered jacket, which is on the table.

One member of the scientific team is about to explain to you the proper manner for putting on and zipping the jacket.

He/she may not touch you or demonstrate this procedure for you (remember that you are blind and cannot see the person); only verbal directions will be provided.

You are to listen to the instructions and do EXACTLY what you are told to do.

Remember that you don't even know what a jacket is!

If you are told to do something specifically (based on the "scientist's" assumption that you know what he or she is talking about) (for example, "Pick up the jacket by the collar" or "Put your hand through the sleeve"), you may actually pick it up by the sleeve and try to put your hand into the pocket since you don't know what a collar or a sleeve is.

Should the instructions seem totally confusing, you may pause, act confused, and scratch your head.

35. I Can Describe That

Time Required 20 minutes

Purpose To provide a means of having learners recognize the importance of saying what they mean and using clear, concise communication skills on the job and in other situations.

Objective(s) Through a lighthearted activity, the facilitator will be able to:

- Demonstrate the importance of verbal communication when sharing information with others; and

- Raise awareness of the difficulties encountered when someone cannot use nonverbal communication or show an item to someone while explaining something (over the telephone, writing email, or traditional correspondence).

Group Size Twenty-four

Process Prior to the start of your session, make copies of Handouts A and B.

Number half of the participants number 1 and half number 2. Have participants form pairs so that there is one number 1 and one number 2 together (if one extra person is present, have him or her join any pair or you can be his or her partner).

Make sure each participant has a pencil.

Have pairs sit in chairs with their backs to one another and tell them they cannot turn around during the activity.

Give all 1's an "A" image handout and all 2's a "B" image handout and tell them not to show what they received to anyone.

Tell learners that the 1's will start when told to begin.

They will have 5 minutes to describe their images to their partners, who will draw pictures (on the backs of their own handouts) of what they hear described by their partners.

After 5 minutes, tell everyone to stop and have the 2's repeat the exercise as the 1's draw.

At the end of the second 5 minutes, have everyone compare the images drawn with the respective handouts to see how closely pictures match originals.

Process Follow-Up   *Ask:* "How many people drew an image that closely resembles the original handout?"

"For those people whose images didn't match the original, why did you have trouble drawing the image described to you?"

"When you were trying to communicate what you saw, what worked well?"

"What did not work so well in communicating your ideas?"

"What questions or thoughts do you have related to the activity and its outcome?"

Give everyone a strip of masking tape and have them place their "master-pieces" on the wall for later review!

Have everyone give a round of applause for the "fantastic artwork."

Give everyone pieces of candy as a reward and to help replenish all the brain cells they burned up through their creativity.

Option   Form groups of three—one communicator, one artist, and one observer.

Follow the same basic guidelines as above except that the third person observes verbal and nonverbal behavior of each person and reports what he or she sees at the end of each round.

At the end of each round, learners should rotate roles so that each group member plays a communicator, an artist, and an observer once.

Props/Tools Needed
- Enough copies of the two picture handouts so that each learner receives the appropriate one;

- Pencils;

- Masking tape to post papers on wall; and

- Candy.

Possible Topic Applications   Any session in which effective interpersonal communication is a desired outcome.

Why It Is Brain-Based   Engages learners visually, auditorily, and kinesthetically;

Involves learners actively;

Stimulates both the left and right brain through language and creativity;

Taps into several of Gardner's multiple intelligences (artistic, linguistic, interpersonal, bodily/kinesthetic, and spatial); and

Involves use of recognition, incentives, or rewards.

I Can Describe That: Handout A

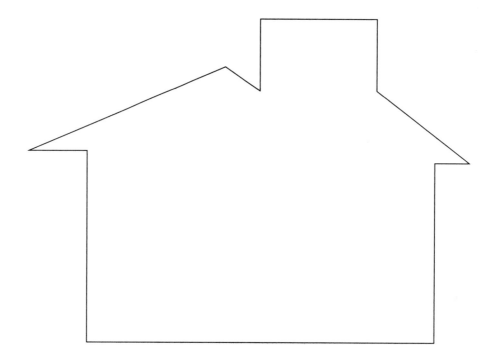

I Can Describe That: Handout B

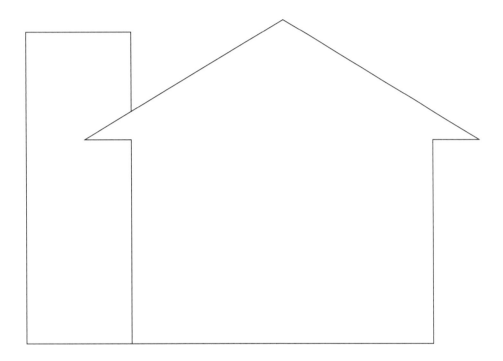

36. Putting Knowledge to Work

Time Required	60 minutes in class, plus on-the-job assessment
Purpose	To immediately provide an opportunity for learners to apply specific course content to the workplace.
Objective(s)	Through use of practical application, the facilitator will be able to:

- Allow learners to reflect on and immediately apply what they learned; and

- Involve learners in reinforcing their own learning.

Group Size	Twenty-five
Process	Following delivery of session content, form equal-sized groups (see Creatively Forming Groups in the Introduction).

Select a leader (spokesperson) and a scribe (note-taker) (see Creatively Selecting Volunteers in the Introduction).

Allow 30 to 45 minutes for learners to work in groups.

Explain that they are to create a bulleted list of key items or points based on program content to consider or address back on the job. For example, if the session is on customer service, some bullet points might include:

- "What is the biggest inhibitor to our attracting more new customers?"

- "How are our policies getting in the way of superior service?"

- "What do our customers typically ask for that we do not currently provide?"

At various points during the activity, sound a noisemaker to regain attention and to check on progress, answer questions, and ensure that learners are on task.

Have scribes transfer their groups' lists to flip-chart pages.

Once the checklists have been developed, have each leader in turn share what was developed with the entire group.

Process Follow-Up Tell participants that their bulleted lists are tools that they can use to go back to their workplace and conduct an actual observation/assessment, based on concepts learned during the session.

Stress that the information learned from the observation/assessment can be shared with appropriate people in their workplace/environment as a catalyst for improvement, discussion, or other appropriate action.

Encourage learners to go back and request meetings with decision makers to discuss the feasibility of conducting an observation/assessment as part of a quality improvement program.

Ask: "What obstacles do you see in conducting an observation/assessment in your environment?"

"How can any obstacles be overcome so that you can successfully conduct the observation/assessment?"

"Who can you enlist in your department/organization to gain approval to conduct an assessment/observation?"

Reward leaders and scribes with candy or small prizes.

Have everyone give a round of applause for their efforts.

Option(s)

1. As part of the Process Follow-Up, you may want to lead a brainstorming activity during which learners identify ways of gaining buy-in from key decision makers in their environments so that the observation/assessment can be done. This brainstorming might also include a list of tools or materials they would need to conduct the observation or other approaches to the process.

2. Instead of a checklist, have learners work in groups to create a worksheet that they can use or have others use in their work environment. Worksheets should be as specific as possible so that information gathered is more valuable and useful. Some possible generic questions or action starters are:

   • "What are some of the causes contributing to. . .?"

   • "What are the obstacles/challenges that might prevent. . .?"

   • "Who are key stakeholders who would benefit from improvement of. . .?"

   • "What tools/materials are necessary for successfully. . .?"

   • "How much time will be required to. . .?"

   • "List ways in which employees/supervisors could improve. . . ."

   • "List specific actions that you can take to overcome. . . ."

3. Instead of a checklist, have learners work individually at the end of a session to create personal action plans for implementation of ideas or concepts learned in the session. Some possible content areas might include:

- "Based on what I have experienced today, I plan to. . . ."

- "To assist me in successfully implementing concepts, I will enlist the help of. . . ."

- "To be successful, I will need the following tools, information, or materials. . . ."

- "Some of the potential obstacles/challenges that I see in implementing what I learned include. . . ."

- "I will do the following to overcome obstacles/challenges. . . ."

- "Other related issues that I need to consider when implementing what I have learned include. . . ."

Props/Tools Needed
- Flip-chart paper;

- Various colored markers;

- Masking tape;

- Noisemaker (bell, whistle, hand clappers, or gong); and

- Candy or small prizes.

Possible Topic Application   Any session in which skills, policies, or processes are addressed.

Why It Is Brain-Based   Reinforces key concepts learned (repetition);

Engages learners mentally;

Appeals to visual and auditory learners;

Involves sound;

Recognizes and rewards learner behavior and efforts; and

Adds color to the learning environment (colored markers).

37. Words to Live By

Time Required 40 minutes

Purpose To provide learners with an opportunity to reflect on workplace issues.

Objective(s) Through the use of commonly known maxims and proverbs, the facilitator will be able to:

- Cause learners to think about how key session concepts might be applied on the job; and

- Help learners process key session concepts in terms of what they mean to them.

Group Size Twenty-five

Process Prior to the session starting, create five different lists of maxims and proverbs selected from the Common Maxims and Proverbs listing at the end of this activity. Each list should have at least five maxims and proverbs on it and relate to your session topic.

Form five equal-sized groups (see Creatively Forming Groups in the Introduction).

Select a leader a (spokesperson, facilitator, and timekeeper) and scribe (note-taker) for each group (see Creatively Selecting Volunteers in the Introduction).

When ready to begin the activity, give one list of maxims and proverbs to each learner. All learners in a given group should receive the same list.

Tell learners that have 10 minutes to go through their lists and match each item to a session concept or idea they learned and that they can apply on the job. For example, "Don't bite off more than you can chew" in a problem-solving session might equate to take on one issue at a time and try to solve it.

Give a 2-minute warning prior to allotted time ending and sound a noise-maker when time is up to regain attention.

Next, tell learners that they have 15 minutes to share what they wrote within their groups and to choose what they believe is the "best" idea from within their groups.

Give a 2-minute warning and sound a noisemaker when time is up to regain attention.

In turn, have leaders share their groups' best ideas with the large group.

Process Follow-Up   *Ask:* "What was the most difficult part of the task? What made it difficult?"

"What was the easiest part? Why was it easy?"

"In what ways did the technique help focus your attention on session content learned?"

"What ideas can you take back and start using in your own environments?"

Reward leaders and scribes with candy or small prizes.

Have everyone give a round of applause for their participation and contributions.

Option   Instead of using this activity for transfer of knowledge, use it as an interim or end-of-session review.

Props/Tools Needed   • Copies of maxims/proverbs; and

• Candy and small prizes.

Possible Topic Application   Unlimited.

Why It Is Brain-Based   Requires learners to match content with something they already know;

Engages learners mentally;

Appeals to visual and auditory learners;

Recognizes and rewards learner behavior;

Uses sound; and

Incorporates novelty into a session.

Common Maxims and Proverbs

A penny saved is a penny earned.

A rolling stone gathers no moss.

A stitch in time saves nine.

Actions speak louder than words.

All that glitters is not gold.

All work and no play makes Jack a dull boy.

An ounce of prevention is worth a pound of cure.

Beggars can't be choosers.

Better late than never.

Better safe than sorry.

Different strokes for different folks.

Don't bite off more than you can chew.

Don't borrow from Peter to pay Paul.

Don't burn the candle at both ends.

Don't put all your eggs in one basket.

Don't rock the boat.

Early to bed and early to rise makes a man healthy, wealthy, and wise.

Every cloud has a silver lining.

Experience is the best teacher.

For every drop of rain that falls, a flower grows.

Good fences make good neighbors.

Good ideas do not drop into closed minds.

He who hesitates is lost.

He who laughs lasts laughs best.

In one ear and out the other.

It is better to light a candle than to curse the darkness.

It never rains but it pours.

It takes two to tango.

It's easier to catch flies with honey than with vinegar.

Keep your nose to the grindstone.

Look before you leap.

Misery loves company.

Nothing ventured, nothing gained.

Out of sight, out of mind.

People who live in glass houses shouldn't throw stones.

Rome wasn't built in a day.

Seeing is believing.

Stone walls do not a prison make.

Success is a journey, not a destination.

The early bird gets the worm.

The grass is always greener on the other side of the fence.

The meek shall inherit the earth.

The pen is mightier than the sword.

Things may come to those who wait, but only the things left by those who hustle.

Too many cooks spoil the broth.

Two heads are better than one.

Waste not, want not.

Well done better than well said.

Where there's smoke, there's fire.

You can lead a horse to water, but you can't make him drink.

You can't judge a book by its cover.

You're barking up the wrong tree.

38. Content Shuffle

Time Required	75 minutes
Purpose	To provide learners with an opportunity to develop ideas for applying session content in their workplace.
Objective(s)	Through the use a small group activity, the facilitator will be able to:

- Cause learners to reflect on session content;

- Cause learners to generate ideas for applying content to their work-place or other environment(s); and

- Tap into the collective knowledge and brain power of small groups.

Group Size	Twenty-five
Process	Prior to the beginning of your session, you'll need to create two different colored decks of 3-by-5 index cards for each group in the activity. You can substitute two different colors of copy paper cut into sections at least 3 by 5 inches.

On one deck of colored cards write the eight to ten key concepts or terms covered in the session—one per card.

On the second color cards write eight to ten of the issues or challenges related to session content—one per card.

For samples, see the lists at the end of this activity. There must be an equal number of cards in each deck, so you may need to include some duplicate concepts or issues, depending on which deck is short.

When ready to start the activity, form equal-sized groups (see Creatively Forming Groups in the Introduction).

Select a leader (spokesperson, facilitator, and timekeeper) and scribe (note-taker) for each group (see Creatively Selecting Volunteers in the Introduction).

Give one of each deck to each group, have them shuffle each deck sepa-rately, then place the decks face down in two separate piles on a table.

Explain that in one colored deck they will find key session ideas or concepts on the cards and that in the other colored deck they will find a workplace issue or challenge related to the session content on each card.

Tell learners that leaders should draw one concept and one issue/challenge card and read both to their respective group (used cards are to be placed face up under the bottom of the appropriate deck once they have been identified).

Scribes will create flip-chart pages with a vertical line drawn from top to bottom dividing the page down the middle. On the top left-hand side they should print the word CONCEPT and on the top right-hand side the words ISSUE/CHALLENGE.

As each card is turned over, the scribe will capture the concept and issue/challenge on the flip-chart page and number them sequentially starting with 1 and going down the page.

After all the cards have been drawn, leaders will take their groups through a brainstorming session to identify each concept one at a time and identify ways in which it can help solve or address its corresponding issue/challenge. Allow up to 60 minutes (no more than 5 minutes per concept/issue/challenge) for brainstorming (time will vary based on actual number of issues/challenge cards were used) and prioritizing items.

As the brainstorming proceeds, scribes should start a second sheet of flip-chart paper with the number 1 and capture different ideas generated by the group for that concept.

After concept number 1 is finished, the scribes should put a "2" on a second sheet, the number 3 on a third sheet, and so on, repeating the process until all the ideas for each concept and issue/challenge have been recorded.

Once all concepts and issues/challenges have been addressed, have groups decide which idea is the most feasible for implementation for each concept, based on known time, resources, staffing levels, and so forth, in their department or organization.

Process Follow-Up   *Ask:* "What worked well during this activity process?"

"What challenges did you encounter?"

"How did you overcome any challenges?"

Go around the room and have each leader in turn present the item his or her group voted as most feasible.

Ask: "Which ideas just presented can you see using right away in the workplace?"

"How will you go about convincing others to buy in on the idea?"

Suggest that each group member should make a copy of all the ideas presented and go back to the workplace/environment to discuss how they might be applied with others in their workgroup or team.

Reward all participants with candy, and give leaders and scribes small prizes for their volunteer effort.

Have everyone give a round of applause for their effort and great ideas.

Option(s)

1. Instead of doing this as a group activity, pass around both decks of cards and have each person choose one card from each deck then individually spend 10 to 15 minutes coming up with ideas for applying the concept to the workplace issue/challenge. Depending on the number of learners present and the total concepts and issues/challenges on cards, you may end up with two or more people receiving the same concept or issue/challenge item. However, because of the random nature of the draw, their content and issue/challenge cards will differ, so their responses and ideas will vary. This will actually result in additional ideas for the group to consider for implementation; or

2. Do this as an instructor-led activity, showing one content item and one issue/challenge, then having the group brainstorm ideas for implementing the concept, which either you or a volunteer captures on a flip-chart page.

Props/Tools Needed

- Flip-chart paper;

- Various colored markers;

- Masking tape;

- Colored 3-by-5 index cards or colored paper;

- Noisemaker (bell, whistle, gong, hand clappers); and

- Candy or small prizes.

Possible Topic Application   Any session in which problem solving, teamwork, and session content review are desired outcomes.

Why It Is Brain-Based   Provides opportunity to reflect on content and workplace issues;

Involves group dynamics and interaction;

Appeals to visual and auditory learners;

Engages learners mentally;

Recognizes and rewards behavior;

Accesses several of Gardner's multiple intelligences (interpersonal and linguistic);

Uses color; and

Includes use of sound (noisemaker).

Sample Card Content

The following concepts and issues/challenges are based on a hypothetical organization at which employees have just attended a session on effective customer service. The concept items are not necessarily specific to the issues/challenges items that are adjacent to them; they can apply to multiple items in corresponding list.

Concepts	Issues/Challenges
Two-way communication	Customer defection
Creating a positive image	Demanding customers
Assertiveness	Rude customers
Nonverbal communication	Unrealistic expectations
Effective listening	Diverse customer base
Effective telephone usage	Technology breakdowns
Personal time management	Impatient customers
Building strong relationships	Changing customer needs

39. What If. . .?

Time Required   60 minutes

Purpose   To provide an opportunity for learners to envision changes in their workplace.

Objective(s)   Through the use of a creative thinking activity, the facilitator will be able to:

- Encourage learners to look beyond traditional paradigms; and

- Help learners generate ideas on how to apply session content to their workplace.

Group Size   Twenty-five

Process   Explain to learners that sometimes we let our own paradigms (ways that we view the world) based on past experiences get in the way of effective problem solving and decision making.

Stress that during this activity they should "let themselves go" and "think outside the box" for ideas that they normally would not consider.

When ready to begin the activity, either show a slide or flip chart listing key session concepts or give out a handout with them on it.

Give learners 3 to 5 minutes to look over the list and think about how these concepts might normally apply to their own workplace.

At the end of 3 to 5 minutes, or when everyone seems to be finished, sound a noisemaker to regain attention. Then have learners take out blank paper and pencils or pens.

Explain that they are going to participate in an activity called "What If. . .?" in which past restrictions (for example, someone saying, "That will never work around here," "We've always done it that way," or "We tried it before and it didn't work") do not exist and are not allowed.

Form equal-sized groups (see Creatively Forming Groups in the Introduction).

Select a leader (spokesperson, facilitator, and timekeeper) and scribe (note-taker) for each group (see Creatively Selecting Volunteers in the Introduction).

Divide the key concepts and assign each group an equal number of them.

Tell learners that they are to brainstorm ways to apply session concepts to their workplace by generating any "What if. . .?" ideas they can think of— no matter how bizarre they may seem. For example, assume you are facilitating a session on effective supervision in which topics like effective coaching, two-way communication, delegation, time management, and dealing with difficult employee situations were addressed. During the session, the issue of high employee turnover might have been brought up. Some of the "What if. . .?" ideas to resolve that issue might include the following (put these on a flip chart for learners to see).

- What if we gave every employee a semi-annual bonus of $500 to encourage them to stay with the organization?

- What if we gave all employees the day off on Fridays to increase satisfaction with the organization?

- What if we allowed employees to take two-hour lunch breaks *every day?*

Have each group spend 15 minutes generating "What if. . .?" ideas.

After each group has generated its list and the scribe has captured each one on a flip chart, group leaders should lead a second round to identify more realistic solutions based on their original "What if. . .?" listing. For example (using the examples above), while you might not have the budget to give everyone a semi-annual bonus, perhaps there is money to provide small incentive prizes (free lunch certificates, movie passes, a parking space close to the building for a week or month) for reaching assigned performance goals. While it is not practical to give all employees Friday off, perhaps you could allow them to come in an hour later or leave an hour earlier on Friday if performance goals are achieved. Additionally, while two-hour lunch breaks are not realistic every day, perhaps you could sponsor a two-hour team lunch provided by the organization once a month to celebrate achievement of goals. Allow 15 minutes for this task.

After all groups have brainstormed their alternative "What if. . .?" ideas and put them on flip-chart paper, have them choose which they think is the most feasible idea for implementation and highlight it on the flip chart.

Have the lists posted on the wall.

In turn, have each leader share his or her group's most feasible idea from the lists.

Process Follow-Up   Following the activity, review the advantages of looking at things from different perspectives (for example, new ideas are generated, old strategies and techniques are changed or updated, people become more creative, motivation improves, and stagnation is avoided).

Stress that sometimes we need a catalyst to think outside the box.

Ask: "What ideas do you see on the posted charts that might be feasible in your own areas?"

"What obstacles do you see in implementing some of these ideas?"

Following this last question, and if time permits, spend a bit of time discussing ways to overcome the obstacles.

Rewards leaders and scribes with candy or small prizes.

Have everyone give a round of applause for all the great ideas and their participation.

Option(s)   1. Use this as an individual activity during which each person takes one or two concepts and on a piece of paper lists as many "What if. . .?" items as he or she can generate. Then randomly request that volunteers read their ideas. Discuss these ideas as a group. Reward volunteers with candy or small prizes; or

2. If time does not exist at the end of the activity to discuss how obstacles might be overcome, have everyone go back and think about this on his or her own. To better ensure that this reflection occurs, have everyone exchange email addresses and have them email their ideas to one another within the week following the session and provide a copy to you. Compile all responses and send them along to departmental supervisors or managers to consider, thus enhancing their perception of return on investment for sending their employees to training.

Props/Tools Needed	• Flip-chart page, slide, or handout with key session concepts; • Flip charts; • Various colored markers; • Masking tape or pins to hang charts; • Blank paper; • Pens or pencils; and • Candy or small prizes.
Possible Topic Application	Any session in which desired outcomes include interpersonal communication, teamwork, problem solving, and session content review.
Why It Is Brain-Based	Taps into left-brain and right-brain processes; Appeals to visual and auditory learners; Causes learners to access memory and recall key session concepts; Engages learners mentally; Recognizes and rewards behavior; Ties to adult learning principles, such as tapping into previous learning and experiences and focusing on problem-centered learning; and Uses color (markers), which can stimulate brain neurons.

40. A Puzzling Matter

Time Required	15 to 20 minutes
Purpose	To engage learners as a team and provide an energizing learning event.
Objective(s)	Through the use of a group puzzle activity, the facilitator will be able to:

- Actively involve learners;

- Provide a vehicle for increased teamwork;

- Facilitate interpersonal communication; and

- Focus on problem solving and decision making.

Group Size	Up to twenty-four
Process	Prior to the session starting, either purchase sets of tangram puzzles for each team or make your own on various colors of paper using the Tangram Template at the end of this activity.

Form equal-sized groups of four to six learners (see Creatively Forming Groups in the Introduction).

When ready to start the activity, give one tangram set to each group.

Explain that the purpose of the activity is to allow learners an opportunity to solve a puzzle as a group within 10 minutes.

Answer any questions they have.

Project the selected tangram image onto a slide screen.

Have learners begin to solve the puzzles and at 8 minutes give a 2-minute warning that time is about to expire.

At 10 minutes, sound a noisemaker or play music to signal the end of time. If additional time is needed, allow 5 more minutes, then signal the end of time.

Check with each group to see which groups accomplished the goal of correct puzzle assembly.

Reward any successful group members with candy or small prizes.

Process Follow-Up	*Ask:* "What was the hardest part of the activity? What made it difficult?"

"What was the easiest part of the activity? How was it easy?"

"How does assembling the puzzle as a group relate to your workplace environment?"

Possible Answers: Requires input from others;

There is a timetable or deadline;

It can be confusing at times;

It is something they have not done before or don't do often.

Answer any questions from learners.

Have everyone give a round of applause for their efforts.

Option(s)
1. Give each learner a tangram and have them work individually. Process the event as described above; or

2. Give half of the learners a tangram and have them work individually and form equal-sized groups with the remainder of learners and have them work on the puzzles as a group. Ask the same questions as above. Discuss the value of pulling from the strengths of others when working on projects. Reward individuals or teams that were successful in assembling their puzzles within the allotted time with candy or a small prize.

Props/Tools Needed
- Paper tangrams or commercial tangrams;

- Ruler (if making your own tangrams);

- Razor or scissors (if making your own tangrams);

- Noisemaker (bell, whistle, hand clapper, clicker, gong, or music); and

- Candy or small prizes.

Possible Topic Application   Any session in which team building, interpersonal communication, problem solving, and decision making are desired outcomes or lessons.

Why It Is Brain-Based   Taps left-brain and right-brain thinking;

Engages learners mentally and physically;

Appeals to visual, auditory, and kinesthetic learners;

Adds an element of competition;

Recognizes and rewards learner behavior;

Adds novelty and fun to learning;

Accesses several of Gardner's multiple intelligences (spatial, interpersonal, linguistic, and bodily/kinesthetic); and

Incorporates color and sound.

Creating a Tangram

1. To create your own tangrams, you can use any material desired. Thicker material (such as colored poster board or construction paper) is typically more durable.

2. Make copies of the tangram shapes on various colors of paper.

3. Cut out the shapes to form sets of tangrams (1 square, 1 parallelogram, 2 large triangles, 1 medium triangle, and 2 small triangles).

4. When cutting the paper, you may want to use a razor or similar tool, if available, so that the cuts are even and not as thick. This helps ensure a better fit of pieces together.

The rules for using Tangrams are really simple. All seven tans must lie flat, they must touch, and they cannot overlap.

The goal is to have learners produce a specific pattern within a set period of time using tangrams.

Tangram Template

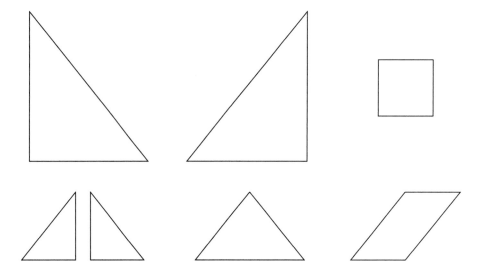

Tangram Puzzles

The following are some possible puzzles that can be projected on a slide for learners to try to solve.

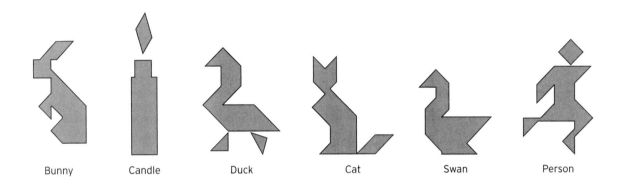

Bunny   Candle   Duck   Cat   Swan   Person

Puzzle Solutions

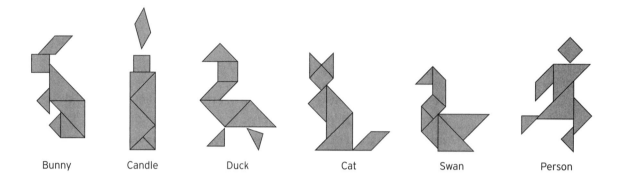

Bunny Candle Duck Cat Swan Person

41. Picture This

Time Required	90 minutes
Purpose	To cause learners from the same team, department, or organization to tap into their creative brains in order to identify issues related to a workplace problem.
Objective(s)	Through a drawing activity, the facilitator will be able to:

- Provide learners with a vehicle to identify elements of a workplace problem they are dealing with; and

- Encourage visualization of various problem-related issues.

Group Size	Up to twenty-five
Process	Form equal-sized groups (see Creatively Forming Groups in the Introduction).

Select a leader for each group (timekeeper and spokesperson) (see Creatively Selecting Volunteers in the Introduction).

Lead a 10-minute brainstorming session during which learners identify key problems or issues (for example, new hardware or software will be adopted, a major policy will change, or a new facility will open) that are currently facing their organization, department, or team as you list their issues on a flip chart. Just create a list; do not discuss the issues/problems.

Give each person one colored stick-on dot, or provide a colored marker, and have them either place their dots or check marks next to the issues they feel are the most important.

The issue with the most dots or checks will be used for this activity. If a tie occurs, toss a coin to select the issue/problem to be discussed.

Give each learner a pencil and several sheets of drawing paper.

Explain that creativity is believed to be primarily a right-brained function and that the right brain is more visually oriented. To tap into this visual side of the brain, they will be drawing images related to the workplace issue or problem identified during the brainstorming session.

Tell them that, working individually, they will have 20 minutes to draw images that represent concerns they have related to various aspects of the issue/problem identified. (For example, with new software or hardware adoption, how will remote locations be networked and how will workers receive any needed training when they are often overwhelmed already?)

Note   You should substitute examples of more appropriate concerns based on the learner group and their environment.

Explain that you will sound a noisemaker as a 2-minute warning before time is up.

Answer any questions, then have learners begin drawing.

Sound a noisemaker at the end of 18 and 20 minutes to signal time is up.

When time is up, have learners get together in their groups to share what they have drawn for 10 minutes.

Sound a noisemaker at the end of 10 minutes to signal time is up.

Next, have each group select one person to compile a list of common concerns from each person's drawing onto a single flip chart, with input from all group members. Allow up to 15 minutes for this compilation.

Sound a noisemaker to signal time is up at the end of 15 minutes.

Have each group leader come to the front and spend 5 minutes sharing what his or her team came up with the rest of learners in the room.

Point out any common aspects that you see identified among groups.

Have group pages taped to the wall for referral during the session and possibly give them to appropriate members of management following training so that action items for addressing the concerns can be identified.

Process Follow-Up   *Ask:* "How did this activity aid you in addressing a key workplace issue?"

"What are some ways that you can see addressing these issues?"

Note   You may want to chart their responses to this question and give the list to management along with the list of concerns.

Have everyone give themselves a round of applause for their efforts and ideas.

Option	Instead of processing the activity as a group, give out sheets of paper and have each learner spend time individually generating ideas on ways to deal with the concerns. Have learners get back into their original groups to share ideas and compile these onto a flip-chart page. Have group leaders present the groups' ideas to the rest of the groups.
Props/Tools Needed	• Colored stick-on dots or colored markers; • Pencils; • Masking tape; • Flip chart or drawing paper for each learner; and • Noisemakers (bell, whistle, or gong).
Possible Topic Application	Any session in which problem solving and creativity are desired outcomes. Also useful in sessions related to change.
Why It Is Brain-Based	Actively engages learners mentally; Taps into the creative right side of the brain; Appeals to visual, auditory, and kinesthetic learners; and Uses sound, color, and learner involvement, which can help stimulate learning.

SECTION 5

Ending on a High Note

"All's well that ends well."

—William Shakespeare

Overview

Experienced trainers and educators have seen how learners seem to best remember what they hear first and last, so it makes sense to ensure that you end your programs in a profound manner. To help ensure that learning was successful and that key concepts were obtained, trainers and educators should give thought to how they will end a learning event.

This section provides a variety of ways to review program content, celebrate learning, and close out a session in a memorable way so that participants walk out with a better understanding of what they learned.

Games and Activities in This Section

42. Verbal Volleyball

Time Required   10 minutes

Purpose   To provide an opportunity for learners to review key concepts learned during the session and celebrate their learning.

Objective(s)   Through use of an end-of-session review activity, the facilitator will be able to:

- Actively engage learners in a review of key session concepts; and

- Allow for individual celebration of learning.

Group Size   Up to twenty-four

Process   Form pairs of learners. Have partners face one another.

Explain that they are going to play "verbal volleyball" in which they will review as many key concepts from the session as they can remember.

Tell learners to decide who will start.

When ready to begin, shout "GO" and the learner designated to start will shout out any key concept, idea, or issue covered during the session.

Partners will then shout out a different concept, idea, or issue, and they will continue volleying the concepts back and forth until they run out of ideas.

Explain that they cannot repeat a concept, idea, or issue already said by a partner.

Once it seems that learners are running out of ideas, shout a 30-second warning and, at the end of that time, sound a noisemaker to indicate time has elapsed.

Have everyone give a "high five" (fingers extended and joined and slapping palms in the air above their heads with their partners) for their accomplishment.

Process Follow-Up	*Ask:* "What do you think some of the most important or beneficial concepts, ideas, or issues we learned today were? Why are they important?"
	Go around the room and have each learner tell one key concept, idea, or issue that he or she experienced and how he or she will be able to use it on the job or in another environment.
	Answer any questions learners have about session content.
	Have everyone give a round of applause for their efforts.
Option	Instead of using this as an end of session activity, you can also use it as an interim review.
Props/Tools Needed	Noisemaker (cow bell, Chinese gong, slide whistle, or bicycle horn).
Possible Topic Application	Any session in which you desire to review key concepts.
Why It Is Brain-Based	Engages learners mentally and physically;
	Causes learners to access memory and recall data;
	Adds a bit of novelty and fun to a review; and
	Adds sound to the learning environment.

43. Pat on the Back

Time Required 20 minutes

Purpose To allow learners an opportunity to review key concepts while sharing compliments with one another.

Objective(s) Through the use of a review activity, the facilitator will be able to:

- Have learners reflect on key session concepts learned;

- Recognize the individual contributions and achievements of their peers during the session; and

- Provide an opportunity for learners to celebrate their learning.

Group Size Up to twenty-four

Process Have learners form a large circle.

Provide someone in the group with a soft, tossable object (Nerf®, Koosh®, or other type of ball or bean bag).

Explain that they have 15 minutes to toss the ball around the circle to one another.

The ball cannot be thrown to someone who has already caught it.

As someone catches the ball, he or she is to shout out one key concept, idea, issue, or thought that he or she has experienced in the session and give a brief explanation of what the concept means.

Each person is also to give the person who tossed the ball to him or her a sincere compliment (for example, "I appreciate the way that you volunteered your experiences during the session" or "Thank you for helping me understand [*concept*] when we were working in small groups").

Continue the activity until everyone has tossed and caught a ball.

If they run out of key ideas or concepts due to the number of participants present, learners can start telling how they will use a key idea or concept once they leave the session.

Process Follow-Up	*Ask:* "What did you learn from this activity?"

Possible Answers: The importance of reviewing key information to reinforce it in your memory; that feedback can be powerful and feel good; that it is important to take time to celebrate your accomplishments.

Have everyone give themselves a round of applause for their accomplishments and contributions.

Option Instead of having everyone in a circle, pass out sheets of paper and have people write down one key concept or idea that they experienced.

Have them also write (print legibly) one compliment for the person to the right (have them write the person's name).

Encourage them to put their names on the sheets.

Collect all the sheets and randomly distribute them to learners.

Ask for a volunteer to stand and open and read what is on his or her paper.

Reward the volunteer with candy or a small prize.

Have everyone give a round of applause at the end.

Props/Tools Needed
- Nerf®, Koosh®, or other type of ball or bean bag;
- Paper and pencil (if using the optional activity); and
- Candy or small prize (if using the optional activity).

Possible Topic Application Unlimited.

Why It Is Brain-Based Appeals to visual, auditory, and kinesthetic learners;

Addresses several of Gardner's multiple intelligences (interpersonal, bodily/kinesthetic, and linguistic);

Addresses personal motivators (for example, need for recognition and social contact); and

Recognizes and rewards behavior.

44. Retention and Reaction

Time Required	15 minutes
Purpose	To provide a process for learners to recognize key concepts learned and to recognize their peers.
Objective(s)	Through an interactive review process, the facilitator will be able to:

- Identify ideas or concepts from a session that learners believe are important;

- Encourage active participation in the review process; and

- Allow learners to provide feedback on their reactions to the session and/or others in the room.

Group Size	Up to twenty-four
Process	When ready to start the review activity, pass out one 3-by-5 colored index card to each learner.

Explain that they will have an opportunity to reflect on key ideas and concepts from the session and capture one of these on their index cards.

Have them turn their cards horizontally and print "Recollection" along the top edge.

Allow a couple of minutes for everyone to write their ideas or concepts and tell them to look up toward you when they have finished so you will know who is still working and needs more time.

After everyone has finished with their recollections, have learners turn their cards over and print "Reaction" along the top edge of the cards and then write one reaction they have to the session (for example, "I came in thinking I knew the content already, but instead learned a number of new strategies" or "I really appreciate the way everyone worked together during the team activity").

Again, ask learners to look up when done.

When everyone has completed the task, ask for a volunteer to read his or her Recollection, tell what it means, and how he or she sees it applying on the job or in other environments.

Reward the volunteer with candy or a small prize.

Continue around the room to the right or left and have others do the same thing.

After all recollections have been reviewed, follow the same format and have everyone read their Reactions.

Process Follow-Up *Ask:* "What do you think the most important concepts were that you learned today? What makes them the most important?"

"What questions do you have about today's activities and content?"

Have everyone give themselves a round of applause for their efforts.

Option(s) 1. Instead of using this as a final review activity, use it as an interim review; or

2. Instead of Recollections and Reactions, have learners write whatever other information you think is important to collect (for example, best thing learned today and biggest challenge using today's information).

Props/Tools Needed • Small prizes or candy;

• 3-by-5 colored (assorted) index cards; and

• Pencils/pens.

Possible Topic Application Unlimited.

Why It Is Brain-Based Appeals to visual, auditory, and kinesthetic learners;

Actively engages everyone in the learning process;

Creates eustress by forcing learners to recall information;

Requires learners to access memory and recall data, then think of applications;

Recognizes and rewards behavior; and

Uses color to enhance the environment.

45. A Postcard to Me

Time Required 10 minutes

Purpose To cause learners to reflect on session content and how they will apply it in the future.

Objective(s) Through a personal visioning activity, the facilitator will be able to:

- Cause learners to immediately reflect on key concepts covered in a session;

- Provide a vehicle for learners to capture key ideas related to session content and think about how they will apply them on the job or in other environments; and

- Ensure program content reflection in the future.

Group Size Unlimited

Process Prior to a session starting, obtain enough 3-by-5 index cards and envelopes large enough to fit them inside for each learner.

At the end of a session, conduct a content review of key session concepts and answer any questions learners might have about the session material.

Pass out one card and one envelope to each learner.

Have each person write his or her name and mailing address on the envelope.

Ask them to reflect on all the key session concepts and choose the one that seemed most important and has the most application to them and their real-world environment(s).

Have learners write the concepts they selected on one side of their index cards.

On the reverse side of their cards, ask learners to write a few ways that they will apply or address the chosen concept once they leave the session.

Also have them list one way that they will know that they have successfully applied or dealt with the concept/issue.

After everyone has finished, have them place their cards in the self-addressed envelopes, seal them, and give them to you.

Explain that they will receive their cards back in the mail in approximately [*number*] weeks.

Stress that when they receive their cards, it will serve as another reminder of key elements of the session and as a checkpoint for them to see whether they acted on their chosen items. It will ultimately allow them to see how the actual outcomes matched their predictions.

Tell them that goals that are written down are typically achieved more often than those that are not.

Depending on the nature of the session, mail the cards back to learners at either three or six months.

Have learners also write their issues/concepts and actions in their handout material so that they can go back to the workplace or other environment and begin working toward achievement of their goals.

Process Follow-Up

Ask: "What challenges do you see in implementing the concept or dealing with the issue that you chose for your card? Why will it be a challenge?"

"How might you overcome these challenges?"

"Who might you approach for assistance in implementing the concept or dealing with the issue?"

Option

Instead of using this as a visioning and review activity, use it as a feedback vehicle on the session. Prior to going to lunch or on a break, give a card to each learner; ask them to write down one thing they have enjoyed or learned in the session thus far on one side of the card.

On the reverse side of the card, have them write one thing that they would change about the session (delivery, format, activities, or whatever) thus far. If nothing, they can write "Nothing" on the card.

Have them give their cards to you prior to going on break; while learners are away, read the cards to see what concepts they have found valuable and to see whether you need to change the delivery style or format of the program. If so, do this as the session progresses.

Reinforce key session concepts when learners return before moving forward with new content, then answer any questions they might have.

Props/Tools Needed

- 3-by-5 index cards; and

- Envelopes.

Possible Topic Application

Unlimited.

Why It Is Brain-Based

Requires memory access and data recall;

Actively engages learners; and

Causes learners to process information and search for additional applications or solutions.

46. We Can Sell This Idea

Time Required	60 to 75 minutes, depending on the number of groups
Purpose	To provide a fun method for learners to revisit key session concepts.
Objective(s)	Through the use of a small group activity, the facilitator will be able to:

- Reinforce key session concepts;

- Actively engage learners in planning how they will apply what was learned;

- Stimulate teamwork; and

- Foster interpersonal communication.

Group Size	Up to twenty-four
Process	Prior to the start of the session, cut out a few hundred print advertisements with photos from various types of magazines (business, hobby, self-help, popular, entertainment, and so on). In doing so, select magazines from different genres (not all sports or fashion magazines).

Gather the following materials together for each group that you plan to have:

- Elmer's glue;

- Scissors;

- Various colors of blank copy paper;

- A variety of colored markers;

- Masking tape;

- Staplers and staples; and

- Rulers

When ready to start, form equal-sized groups (see Creatively Forming Groups in the Introduction).

Choose leaders (spokesperson, facilitator, and timekeeper) for each group (see Creatively Selecting Volunteers in the Introduction).

Give each group an equal amount of the supplies based on the number of team members.

Explain that they are to choose one key concept, idea, or issue addressed during the session.

They have 45 minutes to create a photo advertisement with accompanying text that they might use to convince the person in charge of their organization that they should be allowed to introduce the concept or idea or address the issue chosen.

Tell them that they can examine and select from all of the print advertisements you have collected to determine a layout format and language approach for their advertisement.

They can use as many of the provided materials as they desire to create their advertisement.

Answer any questions that learners might have; then instruct them to begin the project.

Give a 5-minute warning before time expires.

When time is up, sound a noisemaker to attract attention and signal the end of the activity.

Process Follow-Up   *Ask:* "How many of you are pleased with your advertisement? Why or why not?"

"What process did each group use to complete the project? Why did you choose the one you did?"

Have each group leader post his or her group's advertisement, explain what concept, idea, or issue is represented, and tell how it will be used to convince "the boss" to move forward on the objective.

After all advertisements have been shown, have everyone give a round of applause for their efforts.

Discuss the importance of all issues covered in the session and stress the need for them to immediately start applying what they have learned once they leave the session.

Reward leaders with small prizes.

Option	Instead of a print advertisement, have learners develop a creative verbal advertisement that will play on a local station to inform listeners of the importance of the concept or issue selected.
Props/Tools Needed	• Cut-up print advertisements;
	• Elmer's glue;
	• Scissors;
	• Various colors of blank copy paper;
	• A variety of colored markers;
	• Masking tape;
	• Staplers and staples;
	• Rulers;
	• Noisemaker (coach's whistle, train whistle, whistle slider, or cow bell); and
	• Small prizes for group leaders.
Possible Topic Application	Unlimited.
Why It Is Brain-Based	Appeals to visual, auditory, and kinesthetic learners;
	Addresses several of Gardner's multiple intelligences (bodily/kinesthetic, interpersonal, spatial, and linguistic);
	Adds color and sound to the environment;
	Actively engages learners mentally and physically;
	Creates a fun environment;
	Recognizes and rewards behavior; and
	Adds competitive eustress between teams.

47. Content Jeopardy

Time Required	60 minutes
Purpose	To actively involve learners in developing and conducting a game to review session content.
Objective(s)	Through the use of a fun approach to content review, the facilitator will be able to:

- Provide a bit of friendly inter-team competition; and
- Cause learners to recall and act on information learned.

Group Size	Up to twenty-four
Process	Prior to the start of the session, make copies of the Content Jeopardy Rules handout for each team.

Select six major subject categories from the content covered in the session and print each one on a separate sheet of colored copy paper in large letters across the page horizontally (use lighter colored paper so that text will be more visible).

For each of the six subject categories, create five clues in varying degrees of difficulty that will be posted under the category headings at dollar amounts ranging from $100 to $500. For example, in a session on interpersonal communication, under a category heading of "nonverbal cues," the clue might be 7 percent, 38 percent, and 55 percent. The question answer would be, "What are the percentages identified by Dr. Albert Mehrabian's study?"

Next, create five dollar amount sheets showing $100, $200, $300, $400 and $500 values.

Create an answer sheet for use during the game that contains the correct questions related to all clues developed. List them by category and dollar amount for easy reference.

Finally, create a score sheet by listing Team 1, Team 2, and Team 3 at the top of a piece of flip-chart paper.

After all materials have been developed, post the headings across the top portion of a wall or writing surface (for example, a dry erase board), place the dollar value sheets down the left side of the board and put the appropriate clues under each category facing toward the wall so that they cannot be seen by learners (see sample layout at end of activity).

When ready to begin the activity, form three equal-sized groups (see Creatively Forming Groups in the Introduction).

Select a group leader (spokesperson) and scribe (note-taker) for each group (see Creatively Selecting Volunteers in the Introduction).

Give out copies of the Content Jeopardy Rules and verify that everyone is familiar with the rules of Jeopardy®.

Have groups form three lines by team in front of the "game board" with leaders at the front of the lines.

Give each leader a cow bell or other loud noisemaker.

Explain that you will think of a number from 1 to 10 and the group leader guessing it or coming closest without going over starts by selecting the first category and dollar amount.

Once the person selects a category clue, turn it over so that learners can read it.

The first leader to sound his or her noisemaker has an opportunity to provide an answer, in the form of a question.

All of that leader's team members can confer to determine the correct question to a clue.

Play continues with the leader correctly answering a question selecting the next category clue, and so forth until all clues have been disclosed.

Keep track of dollar amounts of the correct answers to determine a winner once the game ends.

At that time, declare a winning team and award small prizes (perhaps plastic trophies) to each member on that team.

If there is a tie, give any additional clue not yet covered and have the leader of the team who knows the answers "ring." Team members may help them with the answer.

If they answer it correctly, they are declared the winner. If not, the alternate tying team gets a chance. Should they also miss the question, toss a coin to determine the winner.

Process Follow-Up

At the end of play, *ask:* "What key concept do you feel will be most helpful for you in the workplace? Why will it be helpful?"

"What challenges do you see in implementing anything learned today? Why will that be challenging?"

"How do you see yourself overcoming any challenges?"

"What questions do you have about anything covered in today's session?"

Option(s)

1. This is a great game for use at the end of a new hire orientation. At the beginning of your orientation, let new employees know that there will be a "test" at the end of the day and that they should take notes and ask as many questions as they like. Throughout the day, provide an interactive exchange of information about company history, benefits, products and services, key management personnel, polices and procedures, or whatever else is important.

   Create your Jeopardy clues and questions based on that content and play the game as described above at the end of the orientation session. This provides an upbeat and fun welcome to the organization; or

2. Instead of using this as an end-of-session review activity, use it as a team-building activity in which learners work in teams to identify six key workplace or other challenges, then develop clues and questions for the game.

Props/Tools Needed

- White and colored paper to create a game board;

- Various colored markers;

- Masking tape;

- Copies of the Content Jeopardy Rules;

- Pencils;

- Small prizes;

- Noisemaker for facilitator (bell, whistle, Chinese gong, or music); and

- Noisemakers for each group (call bell, hand clappers, or finger clickers).

Possible Topic Application	Any session that has at least six major topic headers/sections.
Why It Is Brain-Based	Includes fun;

Adds eustress through competition;

Causes learners to access memory to recall data as they create and play the game;

Appeals to visual and auditory learners;

Involves several of Gardner's multiple intelligences (interpersonal, linguistic, and logical/mathematical);

Recognizes and rewards behavior; and

Enriches the environment with noise and color.

Content Jeopardy Rules

Play commences when one player (selected at random) chooses a category and a dollar amount.

Once the clue is disclosed, any leader can "ring/buzz" in to indicate that he or she knows the correct response.

If the leader ringing/buzzing successfully provides the correct answer (in the form of a question) to the clue disclosed under the dollar amount selected, he or she has to choose another category and dollar amount. A leader's team members may help in determining the correct question.

Any leader can then ring/buzz in, and play continues in the same format until all categories and dollar amounts have been uncovered.

The team with the most money at the end of the game is declared the winner.

Sample Content Jeopardy Board Format

	Category 1	Category 2	Category 3	Category 4	Category 5	Category 6
$100						
$200						
$300						
$400						
$500						

48. Match It Up

Time Required   60 minutes

Purpose   To provide learners with a fun and fast-moving game to review key concepts.

Objective(s)   Through the use of a fun review activity, the facilitator will be able to:

- Actively engage learners in the review of key session concepts; and

- Create a friendly competitive atmosphere in which communication and decision making are employed.

Group Size   Up to twenty-four

Process   Prior to the session beginning, create enough decks of cards using two different colors of 3-by-5 index cards so that each group will have two decks of cards (a set).

On one colored deck of cards, write key terms or concepts from the session. Ideally, you will have twenty or more cards.

On the second colored ("draw") deck of cards, write actual and potential definitions for each of the terms in Deck 1. Create one definition card and two *incorrect* definition cards for each key term or concept.

Note   When creating incorrect definitions, make them variations of the correct definition, but with enough difference to make the answer incorrect.

When ready to start the activity, form equal-sized small groups of at least three, but not more than six, learners (see Creatively Forming Groups in the front of the book) and seat each group around a table.

Select group leaders for each group (see Creatively Selecting Volunteers in the front of the book).

Give each group one set of cards (two different colored decks).

Explain that they are to put the colored deck with the terms face down in the center of a table, with the top card exposed face up on top of the deck so that everyone can see the key concept or term.

The second deck (definition cards) should be shuffled and dealt so that each team member receives five cards apiece. Learners should always have five cards in their hands until the draw deck is exhausted at the end of the game, unless they have forfeited cards for a challenge, as described below.

After definition cards have been dealt, the remainder of the deck (if any) should be placed face down in the center of the table as a "draw" deck.

The goal of the game is for learners to correctly match a definition that they hold in their hands with the concept shown on the table.

Play starts with the group leader and goes to the left.

To start play, leaders will check their cards to see whether they have a definition card that they think matches the exposed concept card on the table. If they do, they will read their cards out loud and claim the concept card. If other group members agree that it is the correct answer, the leader claims the exposed concept card and places it, along with the definition card, on the table in front of him- or herself. This is one pair.

If any group member does not agree that the definition read by the leader is correct, he or she may challenge the definition.

In cases of challenge, the facilitator comes over to decide whether the description was accurate.

If the facilitator agrees that the card is the correct definition for the concept card displayed, the leader may randomly select one card from each group member (without looking at their cards) who challenged the leader's definition.

If the leader does not have the correct definition card, he or she will draw one card from the "draw" deck and, if that is the correct definition, will read it and claim the exposed concept card.

The leader's play ends for that round and the player to the left takes a turn.

Play continues in like fashion until all concept cards have been claimed.

The person with the most matching pairs at the end of the game is declared a winner.

If there are still groups playing at the end of 50 minutes, call time and the players with the most matched pairs are declared the winners.

Read any remaining concepts cards and ask learners to provide the definitions.

Reward winners and leaders with small prizes.

Process Follow-Up   *Ask:* "What concept or idea from today's session do you think is most important? Why is that?"

"Which of the concepts learned in this session will you be able to immediately apply in your workplace or other environment?"

"What questions do you have about anything covered today?"

Have everyone give a round of applause for their efforts.

Option(s)   1. Instead of playing as a group game, form pairs of learners and have them play a card game modeled loosely on the child's game Go Fish®. The goal of the game is to have the most books (four matching cards) at the end of the game.

Prior to the start of the session, create card decks with at least fifty-two index cards that have four each of thirteen key concepts or terms from the session. Each player is dealt five cards, and the remaining cards are placed face down in the center of the table to form a draw deck.

The person with the most of the color blue on his or her body will start first. The starting player can ask his or her opponent for any concept/term card that the starting player is holding in his or her hand. To do this, the starting player will ask, "[*Name of opponent*], do you have any [*concept name*] cards?"

If the opponent has the requested card(s), he or she must give all of the requested card(s) that he or she is holding to the starting player. If the opponent does not have the requested card, the starting player will draw one card from the top of the deck. If he or she draws the concept card requested, he or she may ask for any different concept card. This continues until the first player neither receives the requested card from an opponent, nor draws it from the deck.

The second player then repeats the process of asking for and receiving cards.

When a player has four of any concept card set, it is known as a "book" and these are placed in a stack facing up on the table in front of the player so others can see the concept.

Play continues until at least one player is either holding no more cards or all cards in the draw deck are gone. The player with the most card books on the table at the end of the game is declared the winner.

Reward winners with candy or small prizes.

2. A variation of number 1 above is played with pairs of learners and also loosely follows the rules for the child's game Go Fish®. The goal of the game is to have the most "books" (four matching cards) at the end of the game.

Prior to the start of the session, create card decks with at least fifty-two index cards that have four each of thirteen key concepts or terms.

Each player is dealt five cards, and the remaining cards are placed face down in the center of the table to form a draw deck.

Each pair will toss a coin to decide who goes first.

The starting player can ask for any concept/term cards that the first player is holding in his or her hand. To do this he or she asks, "[*Name of opponent*], do you have any [*concept name*] cards?" All like concept cards being held by the opponent must be surrendered when they are asked for.

When a player asks for a concept card and receives it/them, the requester must then give the correct definition for the concept; if he/she successfully defines the concept, additional cards may be requested until an accurate definition cannot be given, at which time play shifts to the opponent.

If the first player cannot accurately define the concept, the opponent who provided the card has a chance to provide a definition.

If the opponent accurately defines the concept, he or she claims all of the card(s) asked for that the first player is holding; if he or she successfully defines a concept, additional cards may be requested until an accurate definition cannot be given, at which time play shifts back to the first player.

If the opponent cannot define the term either, all the concept cards in question are discarded to the middle of the table next to the draw deck, face up, and neither player can claim them.

If a player asks his or her opponent for a concept card and the opponent does not have a match, the player draws cards one at a time from the draw deck until the requested concept card is drawn.

The opponent then may ask for a concept card like one that he or she is holding. Play continues in a like fashion until all cards have been matched, defined, or discarded and all cards in the draw deck are gone.

Note Any remaining single concept cards being held in a player's hand at the end of the game (because the other three matching cards are in the discard pile), will be added to the discard pile.

The player in each group with the most defined books (four of a concept card type) is declared the winner; if no complete books are held, the player with the smallest number of cards in his or her hand wins.

Reward winners with candy or small prizes.

At the end of the game, ask each pair in turn to read one of the terms/concepts that they could not define, if they have any (from the discard pile in the center of the table).

Anyone in the room can then define that term or concept. You may want to reward learners defining concepts with candy or small prizes.

If no one can define the term or concept, you should provide the accurate description.

3. To reduce time and logistical requirements, put concepts on slides. Give each learner a noisemaker (finger clicker, hand clappers, or bell); as you display a concept, the first person sounding a noisemaker has an opportunity to define the concept or term. If the definition is correct, that person receives a small prize or piece of candy and the review continues in the same manner until all terms have been displayed and defined. If a definition given is incorrect, any other learner can sound his or her noisemaker and attempt to define the concept. Reward successful answers with small prizes or candy.

Props/Tools Needed	• Two decks of different colored index cards;
	• Noisemakers (clickers, hand clappers, or coach's whistles)(option 3);
	• Special 52-card decks (options 2 and 3);
	• Slides (option 3); and
	• Small prizes or candy.
Possible Topic Application	Any session that has enough content to generate the required number of content cards.
Why It Is Brain-Based	Creates a novel and fun environment;
	Ties into previous learner experiences (playing card games);
	Appeals to visual, auditory, and kinesthetic learners;
	Requires learners to access memory and recall information;
	Causes eustress (good stress);
	Recognizes and rewards learners;
	Enriches the learning environment with color and sound; and
	Relates to several of Gardner's multiple intelligences (interpersonal, bodily/kinesthetic, linguistic).

49. Concept BINGO!

Time Required   30 minutes

Purpose   To provide a fun way to review session content.

Objective(s)   Through the use of a variation of the game BINGO, the facilitator will be able to:

- Actively engage learners in a review activity; and

- Create a friendly competitive atmosphere in which communication and decision making are employed.

Group Size   Up to twenty-four

Process   Prior to the start of a session, create the following:

- A blank BINGO Grid (at end of activity) with all the boxes numbered (except the FREE space) based on how many key session concepts and terms you can identify;

- A handout with a list of key session concepts and terms equal to the number of squares on the BINGO Grid; and

- A list of the same key concepts or terms you listed, along with the definition for each concept or term for your own use.

When ready to begin the activity, hand out one BINGO Grid and one key concept/term list to each learner.

Explain that they should write key concepts or terms from their lists in the boxes on their grids until all concepts and terms fill all the boxes.

After everyone has completed their squares, randomly select a concept or term from your definition list and put a check by it so you'll know it has been used.

Read the definition and ask anyone to identify which concept or term it applies to.

If the term is identified correctly, have all learners put an "X" over that concept or term identified.

If the term was not identified correctly, ask for another volunteer.

Continue the process until someone has all the concepts or terms that are in line vertically, horizontally, or diagonally covered with "Xs."

The first person who covers all terms in a line should shout "BINGO!"

After checking the person's sheet, give the person a small prize if he or she is correct, then continue the game until all terms are read and defined.

You can either continue to reward others as they cover their concepts in line or simply tell them after the first learner that, even though someone already won, you will continue the review without prizes.

Process Follow-Up   Following the activity, review any additional key session concepts not selected for the BINGO game.

Ask: "What concept or idea from today's session do you think is most important? Why is that?"

"Which of the concepts will you be able to immediately apply in your workplace? In what way?"

"What questions do you have about anything covered today?"

Have everyone give a round of applause for their efforts in identifying key session concepts and terms.

Option(s)   1. Conduct the activity with teams instead of individuals. Select a team leader for each team (see Creatively Selecting Volunteers in the Introduction). Put the key concepts or terms on slides and project them one at a time as learners "X" them off their BINGO grids. After each concept or term is shown, randomly select teams and ask them to provide the definition for the concept or term. Reward successful team members with candy or small prizes; or

2. Instead of selecting the concepts from a list, put each on a small strip of paper and have learners randomly select each one from a paper bag and read it aloud.

Props/Tools Needed	• BINGO Grids for each learner;
	• List of key concepts for each learner; and
	• Small prizes or candy.
Possible Topic Application	Any session that has enough concepts or terms to fill the BINGO grid.
Why It Is Brain-Based	Adds fun to learning;
	Mentally engages learners;
	Appeals to visual and auditory learners;
	Taps into prior experiences and knowledge (playing BINGO in another environment);
	Requires learners to access memory and recall stored data;
	Recognizes and rewards behavior; and
	Adds an element of friendly competition (eustress).

BINGO Grid

		FREE SPACE		

50. In Summary

Time Required	30 minutes
Purpose	To verify that learners understand key concepts covered in a session.
Objective(s)	Through an interactive group activity, the facilitator will be able to:

- Engage learners in processing key concepts at the end of a session;

- Encourage creativity; and

- Facilitate the exchange of key ideas from the session.

Group Size	Thirty
Process	At the end of a learning event, form equal-sized groups of learners (see Creatively Forming Groups in the Introduction).

Select a leader (spokesperson, facilitator, and timekeeper) and scribe (note-taker) for each group (see Creatively Selecting Volunteers in the Introduction).

Explain that learners will have 15 minutes to create a one- or two-paragraph summary of key concepts from the session that they will share with other teams.

Provide colored markers and a sheet of flip-chart paper to each scribe to capture the final summary points for their groups.

Signal start time and encourage leaders to monitor time.

Give a 2-minute warning at 13 minutes.

At the end of 15 minutes, sound a noisemaker to gain attention and signal end of time.

Ask for a volunteer leader to share his or her group's summary.

Reward the leader who volunteered.

In turn, have each leader share his or her group's summary.

Process Follow-Up	After all groups have shared their summaries, *ask:*

"How did members of your group determine the key concepts to be used in your summary?"

"Were there any additional key concepts that you can now remember that you could not before?"

"How can the concepts learned in this session be applied in the workplace?"

Point out that no one said they could not refer to their notes, if any group mentions that they did not use notes to identify key concepts.

Have everyone give a round of applause for their efforts.

Review any additional key concepts that were not mentioned.

Option(s)

1. Instead of doing a team activity, give each learner a sheet of paper and have them create session summaries that they either share in small groups or with the entire group. Keep in mind that this will take more time for report-outs if everyone is going to share with the entire group; or

2. Do a facilitator-led activity with a flip chart in which learners shout out key concepts and are rewarded for their input.

Props/Tools Needed

- Flip-chart paper;

- Various colored markers; and

- Small prizes for rewards.

Possible Topic Application   Unlimited.

Why It Is Brain-Based   Engages learners mentally;

Adds timed stress, which stimulates the brain;

Incorporates color (markers) and sound (noisemaker);

Encourages creative thinking and problem solving;

Incorporates rewards and appreciation;

Requires reflection and memory recall; and

Uses elements of team competition.

51. The ABCs of It All

Time Required	30 minutes
Purpose	To stimulate recall and reinforce key session concepts at the end of a session.
Objective(s)	By having learners create a listing of key session concepts, the facilitator will be able to:

- Reinforce important learning points from the session content; and

- Engage learners mentally.

Group Size	Twenty-five
Process	Form equal-sized small groups (see Creatively Forming Groups in the Introduction).

Select a leader (spokesperson, facilitator, and timekeeper) and scribe (note-taker) for each group (see Creatively Selecting Volunteers in the Introduction).

Have the scribes take out a pencils or pens and blank pieces of paper and write the letters of the alphabet from A through Z down the left sides of their papers.

Explain that the groups will have 20 minutes to generate lists of key ideas or concepts from the session that correspond with each letter of the alphabet and relate to their workplace. Explain that they can use session handouts to determine these concepts. For example, in a session on supervisory communication skills, the letter "A" might represent, "Ask employees what they think rather than always assuming you know what is best or what they need or want," and the letter "B" might represent, "Begin coaching and sharing information the day a new employee joins your organization and continue it until he or she leaves."

Give a 2-minute warning before time expires.

At the end of the designated time, sound a noisemaker to regain attention and start the process review.

Ask for one group leader to volunteer to give the first letter and the key concept that it represents.

Reward the volunteer with candy or a small prize, then have other leaders in turn offer concepts alphabetically until all letters have been covered.

Process Follow-Up *Ask:* "What did you discover during this review process?"

"How helpful were handout materials in completing this review?"

Explain that this is the value of providing written along with verbal content when they share information with others in order to tap into the visual and auditory learning modalities of people.

Ask: "How can you use the concepts learned during the session on your job?"

"What additional questions do you have related to session content?"

Have everyone give a round of applause for their efforts.

Option(s) 1. Instead of doing this as a small group activity, have individuals take out paper and pencil/pen and do the activity alone; after time has expired, randomly ask for examples of concepts that the letters represent;

2. Use as an opening icebreaker or energizer in any session. Tell learners that they will be creating lists of what they believe are essential elements of [*session topic*]; have learners write the letters A through Z down the left side of pieces of paper.

   Explain that they have 20 minutes to create lists of items related to the session topic (for example, for a session on interpersonal communication, "The ABCs of Effective Communication"). Once the time has elapsed, ask for and reward a volunteer who does a personal introduction and then reads what he or she wrote for the letter "A," followed by a second learner who reads "B" and so on.

   After all letters have been read, have everyone give a round of applause for their great ideas. Present the learning objectives for the session and begin the content delivery; or

3. As a modified form of option 2, at the beginning of a session, try the following: Form small groups (see Creatively Forming Groups in the Introduction); select a group leader (spokesperson) and scribe (note-taker) (see Creatively Selecting Volunteers in the Introduction); provide several sheets of flip-chart paper to each group, along with various colored markers.

   Explain that they have 20 minutes to introduce themselves to group peers and then create a list of items related to the session topic (for example, for a session on interpersonal communication, "The ABCs of Effective Communication").

   Once the time has elapsed, ask for and reward one volunteer leader, who reads what his or her group wrote for the letter "A," followed by the rest of the groups in turn until all letters have been reviewed. After all letters have been read, have everyone give a round of applause for their great ideas.

   Do a quick process review. Present the learning objectives for the session and begin the content delivery.

Props/Tools Needed

- Paper;

- Pencils or pens;

- Candy or small prizes;

- Noisemaker (bell, whistle, horn, or hand clappers);

- Flip-chart paper (if using option 3); and

- Various colored markers (if using option 3).

Possible Topic Application   Unlimited.

Why It Is Brain-Based   Engages learners on a mental level;

Appeals to visual, auditory, and kinesthetic learners;

Adds a level of competition (against other groups and time), which causes the heart to beat faster;

Requires the brain to access memory to recall and apply data; and

Uses rewards.

52. Concentration Review

Time Required	30 minutes
Purpose	To engage learners in a review activity of key concepts learned during a session.
Objective(s)	Through a variation of the game Concentration®, the facilitator will be able to:

- Engage learners in a fun review of key concepts; and

- Introduce friendly competition into a session.

Group Size	Up to twenty-four
Process	Prior to the start of a session, select twelve key terms from session content. For example, in a session on interpersonal communication, you might use "nonverbal cues," "listening," or "verbal cues."

Create a set of twenty-four 5-by-7 index cards that contain twelve pairs of cards with the selected key terms on them (for example, in the example above, you would have two cards with "nonverbal," two cards with "listening," and so on).

Mix all cards so that pairs are separated.

Randomly number all cards on the back sides, starting with number 1 and going through number 24, using colored markers and large bold numbers visible from a distance.

Attach the cards to a dry erase board, magnetic board, or cork board so that they are in rows and in numerical sequence from left to right (see Sample Card Layouts 1 and 2).

Create a flip-chart page to capture team scores during the game and put the numbers 1, 2, and 3 across the top to indicate the three teams that will play the game later.

The rules of the activity are similar to the old game show and board game in that the goal is to discover the location of a matching pair of terms. In this activity, teams play against one another and can collaborate.

Form three equal-sized teams based on the number of learners (see Creatively Forming Groups in the Introduction).

Position teams side-by-side facing the board when ready to start the game.

Randomly decide the order of team play (who goes first, second, and third). This might be done by writing the numbers 1, 2, and 3 on separate sheets of paper, folding them, and randomly distributing them to each team.

Select a team leader for each group (see Creatively Selecting Volunteers in the Introduction).

Explain that, once the game begins, the objective is to find two matching cards on the board by the team leader calling out two numbers (encourage team members to collaborate in determining these numbers).

Learners may not write down the location of terms for reference.

As a team leader calls out a number, turn the corresponding card over and tape it back in the same position so that it is visible to everyone.

Following any unsuccessful guesses, turn the cards back over so that only numbers are showing before the next team starts its turn.

If a team is successful in matching two identical terms, it receives 1 point, those two cards are removed from the board, and the same team is allowed to try again until it fails to find a match.

You can add a bit of complexity and more difficulty to the game by requiring the team that uncovers a matching pair of terms to define or describe the term within 15 seconds for an additional point. If they are unsuccessful in correctly defining the term, either one of the other teams has the opportunity to do so and capture a point.

When a team is unsuccessful, play moves to the next team (team 2 follows team 1, team 3 follows team 2, and team 1 follows team 3).

Play continues until all terms have been successfully paired.

Reward the winning team with candy or small prizes and have everyone give a round of applause for their efforts.

Process Follow-Up   Spend time reading each concept to learners and ask for volunteers to define or explain what they mean. Reward volunteers who provide correct definitions or explanations.

Following the activity, answer any questions that learners have related to session content.

Review any additional key concepts not used in the game.

Ask: "Which of these concepts do you think you will be able to immediately use? Why is that?"

"What questions do you have about anything covered in the session?"

Option   Instead of using the activity at the end of a session, use it as an interim review during the session; follow game rules as outlined in the original activity above.

Props/Tools Needed
- 3-by-5 index cards;
- Various colored markers;
- Flip-chart paper;
- Dry erase board or other surface;
- Masking tape, magnets, or pins (depending on the surface used for attaching the cards); and
- Candy or small prizes.

Possible Topic Application   Unlimited.

Why It Is Brain-Based   Mentally and physically engages learners;

Causes memory access and recall of information;

Appeals to visual and auditory learners;

Incorporates competition (eustress); and

Recognizes and rewards learner behavior.

Sample Card Layout 1

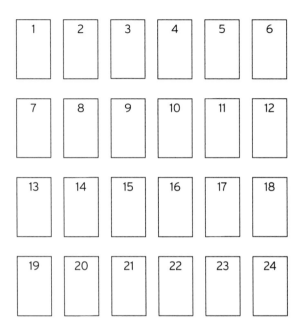

Sample Card Layout 2

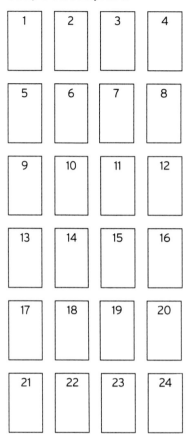

Resources

"Against boredom, even the gods themselves struggle in vain."

—Friedrich Nietzsche

Overview

This section contains organizations, websites, books, music, and much more that can enhance your learning experiences. These resources are offered for consideration and are not endorsed by the publisher or author. The author is president of Creative Presentation Resources and does offer specific guarantees on products, as outlined at www.presentationresources.net.

Due to the fluid nature of the Internet, website addresses listed were active at the time of publication but may change over time.

Information on the following categories is provided:

Suggested Music	Books	Products, Tips, and Free Stuff
Creative Training Products and Seminars	Useful Props and Materials	

Suggested Music

As already mentioned in the Introduction of this book, there are many ways to include music in your sessions. You can use prerecorded classical music or songs that you record yourself from CDs or the Internet. A variety of Baroque, nature sounds, and classical music have been recorded on CDs to specifically use with activities in which the goal is productivity, creativity, relaxation, or fun. You can also purchase songs, television theme songs, and specially created game-show-type music for use in games or other group activities. The choice is yours.

Before using any recorded music for your training or educational sessions, make sure that you know the legal requirements related to copyright. Typically, if you are a teacher of K-12 and in an educational environment, you may not need permission or a license to use music. All other trainers and educators probably will need permission or a license, especially if they are being paid for the program or session that they are conducting. Before using music, it is best that you check Title 17 of the United States Code related to copyright or contact a lawyer or the copyright owner for songs you plan to use to clarify the requirements for usage. The following organizations can provide additional information about music copyright and can assist with providing required licensing:

Broadcast Music, Incorporated (BMI)
10 Music Square East
Nashville, TN 32703
(800) 925–8451
www.bmi.com/licensing

American Society of Composers, Authors, and Publishers (ASCAP)
One Lincoln Plaza
New York, NY 10023
(800) 952–7227
www.ascap.com/licensing

Society of Author's Composers, and Music Publishers of Canada (SOCAN)
41 Valleybrook Drive
Toronto, ON M3B 2S6
(416) 445–8700 or (800) 557–6226
www.socan.ca

The Australian Performing Right Association Limited (APRA)
New South Wales
6–12 Atchison Street
St. Leonards NSW 2065
Locked Bag 3665, St Leonards NSW 1590
Australia
02 9935-7900
www.apra.com.au/

Author's Licensing & Collecting Society (ALCS)
Marlborough Court
14–18 Holborn
London
EC1N 2LE
+44 (0)20 7395 0600
www.alcs.co.uk

Functional Music Recommendations

The following are some possible songs that might be used for adding pizzazz and novelty to your program content.

Openers/Creating a Fun Environment/Energizers

Use the following to wake learners up, before a session or class, while conducting movement or stretching activities, or as transition tunes while learners are moving around.

"Dancing in the Street" (Martha & the Vandellas)

"Eye of the Tiger" (Survivor)

"Fun, Fun, Fun" (Beach Boys)

"Get on Up" (Esquires)

"Goody Two Shoes" (Adam Ant)

"Hokey Pokey" (Kid Rhino/Rhino 4 Kids)

"I Love Rock and Roll" (Joan Jett & the Blackhearts)

"Jump" (Van Halen)

"Octopus's Garden" (Beatles)

"The Chicken Dance" (Werner Thomas)

"The Hustle" (Van McCoy & The Soul City Symphony)

Theme from *Superman* (first movie)

"Walk Don't Run" (Ventures)

"Waltzing Matilda" (Kid Rhino/Rhino 4 Kids)

"What a Wonderful World" (Louis Armstrong)

"Whistle While You Work" (from *Snow White*)

"Whole Lot of Shakin' Goin' On" (Elvis Presley)

"Wooly Bully" (Sam the Sham and the Pharaohs)

"Yellow Submarine" (Beatles)

"Your Mama Don't Dance" (Loggins and Messina)

"Zip-a-Dee-Doo-Dah" (from *Song of the South*)

Festive/Party Atmosphere

Use the following songs when you want to elevate spirits, get the heat pumping faster, and for creating a fun environment.

"Macarena" (Los Lobos or Los Del Rio)

"Twist" (Chuck Berry)

"YMCA" (Village People)

"Electric Slide" (Ric Slide)

"Everybody Have Fun Tonight" (Wang Chung)

"Don't Worry, Be Happy" (Bobby McFerren)

"Footloose" (Kenny Loggins)

"Get Down Tonight" (KC and the Sunshine Band)

"In the Summer Time" (Mungo Jerry)

"Jump" (Pointer Sisters)

"La Bamba" (Ritchie Valens)

"Let's Twist Again" (Chubby Checker)

"Loco-Motion" (Little Eva)

"Louisiana Saturday Night" (Don Williams)

"Neutron Dance" (Pointer Sisters)

"Peppermint Twist" (Joey Dee & the Starlights)

"Pump Up the Jam" (Technotronic)

"Shake Your Booty" (KC & the Sunshine Band)

"Shout" (Isley Brothers)

"Stayin' Alive" (Bee Gees)

"Twistin' the Night Away" (Sam Cooke)

"Wake Me Up Before You Go-Go!" (Wham)

"You Make Me Feel Like Dancing" (Leo Sayer)

"You Should Be Dancing" (Bee Gees)

Teaming/Partnering

Use the following as teams or partners form and relocate or get settled.

"Ain't No Mountain High Enough" (Marvin Gaye & Tammi Terrell)

"It Takes Two" (Marvin Gaye & Kim Weston)

"Lean on Me" (Bill Withers)

"Tel Me Something Good" (Rufus)

"Shop Around" (Smokey Robinson & the Miracles)

"Stand by Me" (Ben E. King)

"That's What Friends Are For" (Dionne Warwick & Friends)

"We Are Family" (Sister Sledge)

"With a Little Help from My Friends" (Beatles)

"Yakety Yak" (Coasters)

"You've Got a Friend" (Carole King & James Taylor)

Visualization/Relaxation

The following types of music are suited for slowing down brain waves and relaxing learners so that they can focus more on visualizing images you suggest.

"Chariots of Fire" (Vangelis)

Classical: Choose slow, melodic sounds (Antonio Vivaldi, Amadeus Mozart, or Claude Debussey), rather than dynamic or major key and upbeat crescendos.

New Age music (Yanni, Enya, David Young, or George Winston)

Goal Setting/Achievement/Closings

Use the following songs as part of end-of-session celebrations or closings or when learners are leaving the room.

"Celebrate" (Three Dog Night)

"Celebration" (Kool and the Gang)

"Glad All Over" (Dave Clark Five)

"Happy Trails to You" (Roy Rogers & Dale Evans)

"Hit the Road, Jack" (Ray Charles)

"Hot! Hot! Hot!" (Buster Poindexter)

"I Feel Good" (James Brown)

"I Just Want to Celebrate" (Rare Earth)

"I've Had the Time of My Life" (Bill Medley & Jennifer Warnes)

"Pomp and Circumstance" (March 1 in D Op. 39 s) (Boston Pops Orchestra)

"School Days" (Chuck Berry)

"School's Out" (Alice Cooper)

"The Best" (Tina Turner)

Theme from *Fame* (Original Soundtrack, "Television's Greatest Hits")

Theme from the movie *Rocky*

"We Are the Champions" (Queen)

BOOKS

Adult Learning, Learning, and Intelligence

Bransford, J.D., Brown, A.L., & Cocking, R.R. (2000). *How people learn: Brain, mind, experience, and school.* Washington, DC: National Academy Press.

Caroselli, M. (1999). *Memory tips for the forgetful.* Irvine, CA: Richard Chang Associates.

Dryden, G., & Vos, J. (1999). *The learning revolution: To change the way the world learns.* Torrance, CA: The Learning Web.

Gardner, H. (1992). *Multiple intelligences: The theory in practice.* New York: Basic Books.

Hayes, E., & Flannery, D.D. (2000). *Women as learners: The significance of gender in adult learning.* San Francisco: Jossey-Bass.

Knowles, M. (1984). *The adult learner: A neglected species.* Houston, TX: Gulf.

Knowles, M.S., Holten, E.F., III, & Swanson, R.A. (1998). *The adult learner* (5th ed.). London: Butterworth-Heinemann.

Merriam, S.B., & Caffarella, R.S. (199). *Learning in adulthood: A comprehensive guide.* San Francisco: Jossey-Bass.

Brain-Based and Active Learning

Dennison, P.E., & Dennison, G.E. (1994). *Brain gym.* Ventura, CA: Edu-Kinesthetics.

Hall, D. (1995). *Jump start your brain.* New York: Warner Books.

Hannaford, C. (1995). *Smart moves: Why learning is NOT all in your head.* Arlington, VA: Great Ocean Publishers.

Hannaford, C. (1997). *The dominance factor: How knowing your dominant eye, ear, brain, hand, & foot can improve your learning.* Arlington, VA: Great Ocean Publishers.

Herrmann, N. (1995). *The creative brain.* Lake Lure, NC: The Ned Herrmann Group.

Ivy, D.K., & Backland, P. (1994). *Exploring gender speak: Personal effectiveness in gender learning.* New York: McGraw-Hill.

Jensen, E. (1995). *Super teaching.* Thousand Oaks, CA: The Brain Store/Corwin.

Jensen, E. (1996). *Brain-based learning.* Del Mar, CA: Turning Point.

Jensen, E. (1998). *Sizzle and substance: Presenting with the brain in mind.* Thousand Oaks, CA: The Brain Store/Corwin.

Pierce, H.J. (2000). *The owner's manual for the brain: Everyday applications from mind-brain research* (2nd ed.). Marietta, GA: Bard Press.

Race, P., & Smith, B. (1996). *500 tips for trainers.* Houston, TX: Gulf.

Rose, C., & Nicholl, M.J. (1997). *Accelerated learning for the 21st century: The six-step plan to unlock your master-mind.* New York: Dell.

Silberman, M. (1995). *101 ways to make training active* San Francisco: Pfeiffer.

Sylwester, R. (1995). *A celebration of neurons: An educator's guide to the brain.* Alexandria, VA: ASCD.

Creativity and Creative Problem Solving

Ayan, J. (1997). *Aha! 10 ways to free your creative spirit and find great ideas.* New York: Three Rivers Press.

Buzan, T. (1993). *The mind map book.* London: Radiant Thinking, BBC.

Forbes, R. (1993). *The creative problem solvers toolbox: A complete course in the art of getting solutions to problems of any kind.* Portland, OR: Solutions Through Innovation.

Higgins, J.M. (1994). *101 creative problem solving techniques: The handbook of new ideas for business.* Winter Park, FL: The New Management Publishing Company.

Leonard, D., & Swap, W. (1999). *When sparks fly: Igniting creativity with groups.* Boston, MA: Harvard Business School Press.

Mattimore, B.W. (1994). *99% inspiration: Tips, tales & techniques for liberating your business creativity.* New York: AMACOM.

Michalko, M. (1991). *Thinkertoys: A handbook of business creativity for the 90s.* Berkeley, CA: Ten Speed Press.

Von Oech, R. (1990). *A whack on the side of the head.* New York: Warner Books.

Creativity in Training

Arch, D. (1993). *Tricks for trainers: 57 tricks and teasers guaranteed to add magic to your presentations.* Minneapolis, MN: Resources for Organizations.

Jensen, E. (1998). *Trainer's bonanza: Over 1000 fabulous tips & tools.* Thousand Oaks, CA: The Brain Store/Corwin.

Jensen, E. (1998). *Super teaching.* Thousand Oaks, CA: The Brain Store/Corwin.

Lucas, R.W. (2005). *The creative training idea book: Inspired tips & techniques for engaging and effective learning.* New York: AMACOM.

Music in Training and Teaching

Green, J. (2002). *The green book of songs by subject: The thematic guide to popular music* (5th ed.). Nashville, TN: Professional Desk References.

Jensen, E. (2000). *Music with the brain in mind.* Thousand Oaks, CA: The Brain Store/Corwin.

Jensen, E. (2005). *Top tunes for teaching.* Thousand Oaks, CA: The Brain Store/Corwin.

Millbower, L. (2000). *Training with a beat: The teaching power of music.* Sterling, VA: Stylus Publishing.

Products, Tips, and Free Stuff

The American Heritage Dictionary. www.bartleby.com/61/. Free online word resource.

Anagram Genius. Create free anagrams using online software. www.anagramgenius.com/

Association for Supervision and Curriculum Development (ASCD). www.ascd.org. ASCD is a non-profit, non-partisan organization that represents educators. Offers free articles and other resources.

Brain Bashes. www.brainbashers.com. Free site for games, puzzles, sudoku, and more.

BrainyDictionary. www.brainydictionary.com/words/ga/game168061.html. A helpful, free online resource for word definitions.

Creative Presentation Resources, Inc. www.presentationresources.net. Free monthly e-newsletter with training and educator tips, articles, games, and activities. Also dozens of free articles for trainers and educators.

Eric Jensen's Learning Brain Expo. www.brainexpo.com. Seminars, conferences, and references on brain-based learning and teaching.

Stinkybear Wordsearch Software Generator. www.stinkybearsoftware.com/. Create free word-search puzzles, download to Microsoft® Word, and use for non-commercial purposes.

Wordsmith. www.wordsmith.org/anagram/index.html. Free site for scrambling words into anagrams (word puzzles).

Creative Training Products and Seminars

Creative Presentation Resources, Inc.

P.O. Box 180487

Casselberry, FL 32718–0487

(800) 308–0399/(407) 695–5535

www.presentationresources.net

Online resource for over one thousand creative games, toys, books, training and teaching aids, and equipment for trainers, educators, presenters, and schools. Creative training and train-the-trainer programs. Free training and education articles for use in learning environments.

Badge a Minit

345 North Lewis Avenue

Oglesby, IL 61348

(815) 883–9696

(800) 223–4103

www.badgeaminit.com

Button/badgemaking equipment and supplies for creating custom-themed badges as incentives for games and activities.

Active Training

www.activetraining.com/

303 Sayre Drive

Princeton, NJ 08540

(800) 924–8157

Train-the-trainer workshops.

The Bob Pike Group

www.bobpikegroup.com

7620 West 78th Street

Edina, MN 55439

(952) 829–1954

(800) 383–9210

Seminars and workshops on creative training techniques.

The Center for Accelerated Learning

1103 Wisconsin Street

Lake Geneva, WI 53147

(262) 248–7070

Products and tips for accelerated learning.

The Thiagi Group

www.thiagi.com

4423 E. Trailridge Road

Bloomington, IN 47408–9633

(812) 332–1478

Workshops, articles, newsletter, and game-related products. Source for workshops, articles, and resources related to games, activities, and experiential learning.

Useful Props and Materials

The following items may be obtained at various toy and teacher supply stores and at Creative Presentation Resources (www.presentationresources.net) or by calling (800) 308–0399/ (407) 695–5535.

Attention Getters

Bicycle horn

Chinese gong

Clicker

Coach's whistle

Cow bell

Mooing cow

Music based on session topic and theme (see Functional Music Suggestions)

Plastic hand clapper (7-inch or 15-inch)

Slide whistle

Smile face laughing bag

Squawkin' chicken

Teacher's classroom bell

Train whistle

Tambourine

General Props

Animal noses

Arrow through the head

Double-roll coupons

Funny hats

Groucho glasses

Hollywood clapboard

Needle through the balloon

Grouping Items

Colored office stickers

Themed erasers

Themed pencils

Themed stickers

Toy animals and figures

Incentives/Prizes

Squeezable foam toys:

Apples

Blob balls

Brains stars

Earth balls

Koosh® balls

Puffer balls

Smile-face balls

Tooth

Other smile-face items (balls, pencil sharpeners, pencils, puzzles, or erasers)

References

Gardner, H. (1993). *Multiple intelligences: The theory in practice.* New York: Basic Books.

Howard, P.J. (2006). *The owner's manual for the brain: Everyday applications from the mind-brain research* (3rd ed.). Atlanta, GA: Bart Press.

Jensen, E., (2000). *Music with the brain in mind.* San Diego, CA: The Brainstore/Corwin Press.

Jensen, E. (2005). *Top tunes for teaching.* San Diego, CA: The Brain Store/Corwin Press.

Millbower, L. (2000). *Training with a beat.* Sterling, VA: Stylus Publishing.

Rauscher, F., & Ky, K. (1993). Music and spatial task performance. *Nature, 365,* 611.

Yaman, D., & Covington, M. (2006). *I'll take learning for 500: Using game shows to engage, motivate, and train.* San Francisco, CA: Pfeiffer.

About the Author

BOB LUCAS holds dual roles as president of Creative Presentation Resources—a creative training and products company—and as a founding managing partner for Global Performance Strategies, LLC—an organization specializing in performance-based training, consulting services, and life planning seminars.

Bob has extensive experience in human resources development, management, and customer service over the past three decades in a variety of organizational environments. This background gives him a real-world perspective on the application of theory he has studied and used for several decades. He is certified in a variety of programs from various national and international training organizations.

Bob focuses on assisting organizations and individuals to develop innovative and practical strategies for improved workplace performance. His areas of expertise include presentation skills, training and management program development, train-the-trainer, interpersonal communication, adult learning, diversity, customer service, and employee and organization development.

Currently, Bob serves on the board of directors for the Central Florida Safety Council. Additionally, he was formerly the president of the Central Florida Chapter of the American Society for Training and Development and served on the board for the Metropolitan D.C. and Suncoast chapters of that organization.

In addition to giving regular presentations to various local and national groups and organizations, Bob has served as an adjunct faculty member for Webster University in Orlando since 1994. In that position, he teaches organizational and interpersonal communication, introduction to HRD, diversity, and training and development.

Listed in *Who's Who in the World, Who's Who in America,* and *Who's Who in the South & Southeast* for a number of years, Bob is also an avid writer. Published works include *People Strategies for Trainers: 176 Tips & Techniques for Dealing with Difficult Classroom Situations; The Creative Training Idea Book: Inspired Tips & Techniques for Engaging and Effective Learning; The BIG Book of Flip Charts; How to Be a Great Call Center Representative; Customer Service Skills & Concepts for Success; Customer Service: Building Successful Skills for the 21st Century* (3rd ed.); *Job Strategies for New Employees; Communicating One-to-One: Making the Most of Interpersonal Relationships; Coaching Skills: A Guide for Supervisors; Effective Interpersonal Skills; Training Skills for Supervisors;* and *Customer Service: Skills and Concepts for Business.*

Additionally, he has been a contributing author to fourteen other compilation publications for Jossey-Bass/Pfeiffer, ASTD, and HRD Press.

Bob has earned a bachelor of science degree in law enforcement from the University of Maryland and a master of arts degree with a focus in human resource development from George Mason University in Fairfax, Virginia. He is currently enrolled in the master of arts program in management at Webster University.

Pfeiffer Publications Guide

This guide is designed to familiarize you with the various types of Pfeiffer publications. The formats section describes the various types of products that we publish; the methodologies section describes the many different ways that content might be provided within a product. We also provide a list of the topic areas in which we publish.

FORMATS

In addition to its extensive book-publishing program, Pfeiffer offers content in an array of formats, from fieldbooks for the practitioner to complete, ready-to-use training packages that support group learning.

FIELDBOOK Designed to provide information and guidance to practitioners in the midst of action. Most fieldbooks are companions to another, sometimes earlier, work, from which its ideas are derived; the fieldbook makes practical what was theoretical in the original text. Fieldbooks can certainly be read from cover to cover. More likely, though, you'll find yourself bouncing around following a particular theme, or dipping in as the mood, and the situation, dictate.

HANDBOOK A contributed volume of work on a single topic, comprising an eclectic mix of ideas, case studies, and best practices sourced by practitioners and experts in the field.

An editor or team of editors usually is appointed to seek out contributors and to evaluate content for relevance to the topic. Think of a handbook not as a ready-to-eat meal, but as a cookbook of ingredients that enables you to create the most fitting experience for the occasion.

RESOURCE Materials designed to support group learning. They come in many forms: a complete, ready-to-use exercise (such as a game); a comprehensive resource on one topic (such as conflict management) containing a variety of methods and approaches; or a collection of like-minded activities (such as icebreakers) on multiple subjects and situations.

TRAINING PACKAGE An entire, ready-to-use learning program that focuses on a particular topic or skill. All packages comprise a guide for the facilitator/trainer and a workbook for the participants. Some packages are supported with additional media—such as video—or learning aids, instruments, or other devices to help participants understand concepts or practice and develop skills.

- *Facilitator/trainer's guide* Contains an introduction to the program, advice on how to organize and facilitate the learning event, and step-by-step instructor notes. The guide also contains copies of presentation materials—handouts, presentations, and overhead designs, for example—used in the program.

• *Participant's workbook* Contains exercises and reading materials that support the learning goal and serves as a valuable reference and support guide for participants in the weeks and months that follow the learning event. Typically, each participant will require his or her own workbook.

ELECTRONIC CD-ROMs and web-based products transform static Pfeiffer content into dynamic, interactive experiences. Designed to take advantage of the searchability, automation, and ease-of-use that technology provides, our e-products bring convenience and immediate accessibility to your workspace.

METHODOLOGIES

CASE STUDY A presentation, in narrative form, of an actual event that has occurred inside an organization. Case studies are not prescriptive, nor are they used to prove a point; they are designed to develop critical analysis and decision-making skills. A case study has a specific time frame, specifies a sequence of events, is narrative in structure, and contains a plot structure—an issue (what should be/have been done?). Use case studies when the goal is to enable participants to apply previously learned theories to the circumstances in the case, decide what is pertinent, identify the real issues, decide what should have been done, and develop a plan of action.

ENERGIZER A short activity that develops readiness for the next session or learning event. Energizers are most commonly used after a break or lunch to stimulate or refocus the group. Many involve some form of physical activity, so they are a useful way to counter post-lunch lethargy. Other uses include transitioning from one topic to another, where "mental" distancing is important.

EXPERIENTIAL LEARNING ACTIVITY (ELA) A facilitator-led intervention that moves participants through the learning cycle from experience to application (also known as a Structured Experience). ELAs are carefully thought-out designs in which there is a definite learning purpose and intended outcome. Each step—everything that participants do during the activity—facilitates the accomplishment of the stated goal. Each ELA includes complete instructions for facilitating the intervention and a clear statement of goals, suggested group size and timing, materials required, an explanation of the process, and, where appropriate, possible variations to the activity. (For more detail on Experiential Learning Activities, see the Introduction to the *Reference Guide to Handbooks and Annuals*, 1999 edition, Pfeiffer, San Francisco.)

GAME A group activity that has the purpose of fostering team spirit and togetherness in addition to the achievement of a pre-stated goal. Usually contrived—undertaking a desert expedition, for example—this type of learning method offers an engaging means for participants to demonstrate and practice business and interpersonal skills. Games are effective for team building and personal development mainly because the goal is subordinate to the process—the means through which participants reach decisions, collaborate, communicate, and generate trust and understanding. Games often engage teams in "friendly" competition.

ICEBREAKER A (usually) short activity designed to help participants overcome initial anxiety in a training session and/or to acquaint the participants with one another. An icebreaker can be a fun activity or can be tied to specific topics or training goals. While a useful tool in itself, the icebreaker comes into its own in situations where tension or resistance exists within a group.

INSTRUMENT A device used to assess, appraise, evaluate, describe, classify, and summarize various aspects of human behavior. The term used to describe an instrument depends primarily on its format and purpose. These terms include survey, questionnaire, inventory, diagnostic, survey, and poll. Some uses of instruments include providing instrumental feedback to group members, studying here-and-now processes or functioning within a group, manipulating group composition, and evaluating outcomes of training and other interventions.

Instruments are popular in the training and HR field because, in general, more growth can occur if an individual is provided with a method for focusing specifically on his or her own behavior. Instruments also are used to obtain information that will serve as a basis for change and to assist in workforce planning efforts.

Paper-and-pencil tests still dominate the instrument landscape with a typical package comprising a facilitator's guide, which offers advice on administering the instrument and interpreting the collected data, and an initial set of instruments. Additional instruments are available separately. Pfeiffer, though, is investing heavily in e-instruments. Electronic instrumentation provides effortless distribution and, for larger groups particularly, offers advantages over paper-and-pencil tests in the time it takes to analyze data and provide feedback.

LECTURETTE A short talk that provides an explanation of a principle, model, or process that is pertinent to the participants' current learning needs. A lecturette is intended to establish a common language bond between the trainer and the participants by providing a mutual frame of reference. Use a lecturette as an introduction to a group activity or event, as an interjection during an event, or as a handout.

MODEL A graphic depiction of a system or process and the relationship among its elements. Models provide a frame of reference and something more tangible, and more easily remembered, than a verbal explanation. They also give participants something to "go on," enabling them to track their own progress as they experience the dynamics, processes, and relationships being depicted in the model.

ROLE PLAY A technique in which people assume a role in a situation/scenario: a customer service rep in an angry-customer exchange, for example. The way in which the role is approached is then discussed and feedback is offered. The role play is often repeated using a different approach and/or incorporating changes made based on feedback received. In other words, role playing is a spontaneous interaction involving realistic behavior under artificial (and safe) conditions.

SIMULATION A methodology for understanding the interrelationships among components of a system or process. Simulations differ from games in that they test or use a model that depicts or mirrors some aspect of reality in form, if not necessarily in content. Learning occurs by studying the effects of change on one or more factors of the model. Simulations are commonly used to test hypotheses about what happens in a system—often referred to as "what if?" analysis—or to examine best-case/worst-case scenarios.

THEORY A presentation of an idea from a conjectural perspective. Theories are useful because they encourage us to examine behavior and phenomena through a different lens.

TOPICS

The twin goals of providing effective and practical solutions for workforce training and organization development and meeting the educational needs of training and human resource professionals shape Pfeiffer's publishing program. Core topics include the following:

Leadership & Management

Communication & Presentation

Coaching & Mentoring

Training & Development

E-Learning

Teams & Collaboration

OD & Strategic Planning

Human Resources

Consulting

What will you find on pfeiffer.com?

- The best in workplace performance solutions for training and HR professionals

- Downloadable training tools, exercises, and content

- Web-exclusive offers

- Training tips, articles, and news

- Seamless on-line ordering

- Author guidelines, information on becoming a Pfeiffer Affiliate, and much more

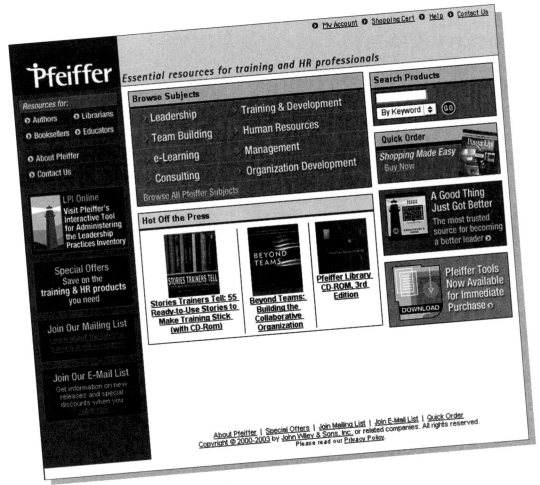

Discover more at www.pfeiffer.com